Is the
Long Island
Medium
the Real Deal?

KIRBY ROBINSON

Copyright © 2013 Kirby Robinson

All rights reserved.

ISBN:149103808X
ISBN-13: 978-1491038086

Disclaimer:

The information in this book was gathered from various sources. Although the author and publisher have made every effort to ensure that the information in this book was correct at press time, the author and publisher do not assume and hereby disclaim any liability to any party for any loss, damage, or disruption caused by errors or omissions, whether such errors or omissions result from negligence, accident, or any other cause.
If you wish to reproduce any part of this book, you must request permission in advance, as the material is protected under copyright law.
All requests must be made via email to:
freeallspirits@live.com

DEDICATION

I would like to dedicate this book to:

~ All my new age teachers and my mentor that helped me manifest my fake psychic abilities. If it hadn't been for them and the great job they did teaching me all the lies of the new age, I wouldn't be able to teach the public not to buy into the lies. God is far smarter than anyone associated with the new age.

~ Daniel and Ezekiel -- two of the greatest prophets in the Old Testament.

~ The greatest prophet of all time my Lord Jesus Christ. His death gives me the ability to stand up to the growing army of darkness out there, as the new age lies and deceptions keep growing in these spiritually troubled times.

CONTENTS

	Introduction	i
1	Back into the Fire	7
2	Why Psychics are Dangerous	17
3	Trying to Make Sense of Psychic Nonsense	41
4	Have We Seen a Real Reading from Theresa?	53
5	The Science of Cold Readings	61
6	An Audience Reading from Theresa Caputo	69
7	Past Life Regression – Real or Not?	76
8	Theresa Takes on the Sunshine State	80
9	Misinformation in the Land of [Dr.] Oz	92
10	Plants in the Spotlight	99
11	Live with Theresa Caputo in Cerritos, CA	103
12	Who is Spirit?	110
13	Does Theresa Cause Harm?	120
14	Confusion	127
15	Final Thoughts	135
16	About the Author	139

INTRODUCTION

Here we go again!

It's four o'clock in the morning.

The last time I wrote about being awake at four a.m., it was for the introduction of my last book *Never Mock God: An Unauthorized Investigation into Paranormal State's 'I Am Six' Case*. Now, I'm about to put pen to paper once again. This time it has nothing to do with *Paranormal State*. No fake Episcopal priests or deluded young women seeking love from a fake para-celebrity.

I take a sip of Dr Pepper. Too many cups of coffee consumed over a long hard day of dealing with the dark forces that live in the shadow world. Just because you can't see them doesn't mean they aren't there. It doesn't mean they can't terrorize you, your home, your family, and loved ones. It doesn't mean that if it gets bad enough they will take your life and claim your soul.

What dark creatures am I talking about? Demons. They love to inflict pain on people but the media gives a distorted view of how they actually operate in the spiritual realm. They just don't drop into your life unless you make an invitation for them to haunt and torment you. What can serve as an invitation?

- Not being saved

- Use of hallucinogenic drugs

- Over consumption of alcohol

- Dabbling in the dark arts

- A family history of taking part of the dark arts

- Casting a curse

- Dabbling in a false religion

- Inviting spirits into your home

- Having a psychic or psychic/medium perform spirit communication for you

- Having a psychic/medium perform a healing on you

- Having a psychic/medium assist you with guided mediation or past-life regression

The last three reasons are the most common cause for people to find out they have a demonic infestation--and that concerns me.

I've been on the other side of the table as a psychic. I know as much as the best of them. I can talk new age jargon as well as anyone in the field. I used to think that this was the path to helping people, but now I realize I was wrong. There is only one person that can help people with issues of a spiritual nature and that is the Lord Jesus Christ. I can't help anyone, nor can any psychic--real or fake.

The case I just wrapped up concerned a family that hosted a birthday party for a woman who turned 30. Just for kicks they hired a psychic-medium to come to their home and do what some might call a group reading, or a gallery reading. Whatever you call it, it was the start of a nightmare for the family and some of the other partygoers.

That psychic brought along his spirit guides, angels and dozens of spirits of the dead that had messages for those attending. All those and more were given free rein to enter the home of someone who was doing nothing more than celebrating a birthday.

Claiming they were peaceful and loving angels and spirit guides, the psychic actually brought along his demons. Because they had an invitation to attend that birthday party, they never left. Long after the psychic had departed, they remained. Well, aside from some of the demons who attached themselves to a few of the other party attendees and went home with them.

Within weeks, furniture started to move around rooms. Doors opened and closed. Lights flickered and in several cases light bulbs exploded. Cold spots were felt and the furnace couldn't maintain a steady temperature. The family heard screams and worse – day and night. A foul stench permeated the home. Family members got sick. Grape juice turned to wine. Wine changed into something that looked and smelled like blood. The family turned to the internet for help after their local church refused to assist them. The pastor actually told the family to bring back the psychic to get help! Luckily, they found me, and I was able to do a complete investigation. I went into the home with the Armor of God on and through His Word drove the demonic out. Then I went to the homes of those who attended the party and had brought demons home with them.

I sit at the table in the motel room hoping it was over but knowing that it wasn't. Something was just outside the room screaming and cursing every hateful sentiment at the top of its voice. Luckily, you had to be able to tune into the spiritual realm to hear such blasphemy. If everyone at the motel could have heard it, there would have been quite an uproar.

What was the name of the demon? That will be revealed later.

What about the psychic? I had a reading done with the psychic-medium. He did nothing more than a cold reading, just guessing at whom I had in the spirit world. Without mincing words, the psychic was fake. But it doesn't matter. Usually, a fake psychic will tell that lie about being real so often that they start to think they are. Eventually, they really start to see things and hear spirits. This is because the demon[s] will feed into the lie.

Fake psychics can do as much damage as real psychics. In addition, those "real" psychics are only real in the sense that they are talking to someone--it's just not who they think it is.

Lately it seems that we have never been as seduced by psychics/mediums/healers and those who practice false new age teachings. Every place you turn psychics are being promoted, whether through Facebook, the rest of the net, TV, magazines and books. Phone psychics are still being promoted on late night TV, in newspapers, and websites like Psychic Source, Hollywood Psychics, California Psychics, and Ask Now. All these sites along with many others do a thriving business.

The newly crowned queen of such things is Theresa Caputo, the *Long Island Medium*. Her hit show on TLC, [The Learning Channel] is a network that used to focus on education and learning. That changed about a decade ago, and its offerings consist of such "reality" shows as *Toddlers & Tiaras*, *19 Kids and Counting*, and *Here Comes Honey Boo Boo*.

Long Island Medium focuses on Theresa's life at home with her husband Larry, son Larry Jr., and daughter Victoria--who has recently gone away to college. We see the peppy blonde SUV-driving Theresa as she buzzes around the Hicksville, New York area on her way to group readings or does private readings in her comfortable suburban home. As though further proving her mediumship abilities, Mrs. Caputo does spontaneous readings in public places with total strangers.

Are her claims real? Are her talents real? Is everything faked to get ratings and make her the number one medium in America? Is God in His Heaven giving the healing messages that Theresa is spouting? Or is she receiving her information from the powerful dark master who is set on seducing the public and leading them away from the path?

CHAPTER 1
BACK INTO THE FIRE

"What right do you have to say anything about *Paranormal State*? Were you there during filming? And who the hell are you anyway?"

"Chip Coffey is the most legit psychic-medium that has ever lived. You're just jealous."

"Ryan Buell and Chip Coffey are men of God. You're not so just shut up."

The above quotes are some examples of the kind and loving emails sent to me after my books were released. My books focused on the antics of the Paranormal Research Society [PRS] and their A&E show *Paranormal State*. One of the regular guests on the show for the first few seasons was a psychic-medium by the name of Chip Coffey. He also wrote a book entitled *Growing Up Psychic: My Story of Not Just Surviving but Thriving--and How Others Like Me Can, Too*.

I even got hate emails and threats over a book that I didn't write! It's called *Psychic Kids: Children of the Paranormal: Fact or Fake?* The book was about the numerous claims Mr. Coffey made in his own book on the subject of so-called psychic kids.

One takes that risk when kicking stones best left unkicked and shaking branches best left unshaken. Yet some of us can't help looking under rocks, shaking branches, stirring up the water, and spitting into the wind.

WHY ME?

The story starts many years ago in the hills and hollers of Southern Indiana. I grew up in Paragon, population 300. John Dillinger is rumored to have robbed the only bank in town back in the 1930s. In nearby Martinsville, Bobby Helms, the composer of the song *Jingle Bell Rock,* was born and raised.

I was a different sort of child. I began speaking when I was four-years-old and tended to stay by myself. It's not that I didn't have friends, or that I was unable or unwilling to talk. I had friends, but others couldn't see them. I spent many hours talking to them and learning from them.

The people I saw were all ages and races. There were even children and a few babies [they would never stop crying!]. These people spoke English, as we'd expect to hear it spoken in my area. Others spoke it with thick accents that years later I would learn were from England, Ireland, and Australia. Some spoke with European accents and others spoke no English at all. I saw people with brown skin, white skin, and the black skin of those I'd later learn lived in Africa and Southern India. I saw individuals who wore nothing more than loincloths. Some of the visitors wore contemporary clothing, while others dressed as if they lived hundreds, if not thousands, of years ago.

The visitors talked to me as if they were there. They listened as I spoke and reacted to what I said. Many spoke of things I didn't understand and still don't. When a foreign language was spoken at first I didn't understand but as time went by I started to.

Paragon wasn't even a one-stoplight town until the mid 1970s. The big thing in town was watching the leaves fall and the signs change at the local IGA market. Foreign languages weren't spoken. There were four local TV channels: NBC, CBS, ABC and a channel from Indianapolis 40 miles away. I'd never heard of PBS until I was in high school, so being exposed to such things was unlikely. When I began hearing Chinese, Japanese, Tibetan, French, German etc., I knew what it was without others telling me.

I saw images of the Hindu gods, Buddha, and even the female Buddha, Tara. I may not have known who they were, but I knew what they were.

I was always shocked that other people couldn't see or hear them so I learned not to talk about them. I never forgot about them and always knew it was important to listen and learn.

I didn't learn to read until I was in sixth grade. Not that I wasn't reading, I was. I was reading books others couldn't see. When I did start to read, I absorbed books about cowboys and adventure books. I consumed books on UFO's, ghosts, Atlantis, ESP, and ancient religions.

Along with the spirits of humans, something dark

and wicked would come around after dark or during stormy or long winter nights. Then I felt the heavy breath, heard the grinding of teeth, and was filled with a sense of evil. These evil entities talked to me, but never about things I wanted to hear.

My family was Christian. We owned a big Bible but you never saw anyone read it. Church attendance was sporadic, usually during times of trouble or on the two big holidays: Christmas and Easter. I never heard about the Blood of Jesus, the Cross, the Holy Spirit, the casting out of demons, or the spiritual gifts.

Just by chance, I learned that when these things [I later learned they were demons] came around, if I said in the name of God or "Dear God--get away!" they would depart. They never want far away, I couldn't see them, but I knew they were there.

Every time I tried to walk away from the spiritual connection that I had, every time I tried to say I'm able to live without it, I always ended up embracing it. It seemed like I could find no emotional peace or contentment when I was away from the spiritual realm. As soon as I opened up the floodgates, that harmony would return. At that time in my life I didn't understand the idea of spiritual seduction which is a tool that is often used by demons/dark forces to bring the unsuspecting [those who don't believe in evil]. If I hadn't accepted Christ and later rebuked all the works of Satan, I would've been totally seduced by all things spiritually evil.

A psychic who hangs out on Facebook claims that he was the first human answering machine. He could look at a phone and it would ring. [I guess there are lots of human answering machines. If you look at a phone long enough it'll ring whether you're psychic or not.] When the phone rang, I could tell who it was. Deaths and bad news would end up in my mind prior to being told. News events played in my dreams before the next day's news. Nothing could drown it out, not even the whiskey I drank the next day. That bad news would be there -- sometimes stronger than ever.

I decided if it couldn't be turned off then I'd better accept it and live with it. I turned to God as I started to read in the Bible about the spiritual gifts of healing, speaking in tongues and speaking words of prophecy, which we'll show later in this book is quite different than giving a psychic prediction.

I was attending a teaching by Dr. Lester Sumrall, a pastor, and a true man of God who had been so blessed by Jesus. Lester and his family have touched so many -- and still do today.

He was a friend and always had time to talk to me. Dr. Sumrall told me I should be a preacher and attend an evangelistic school, and then go on the road to teach the world about Jesus. I told him that was not for me but it also seemed that when we talked the subject of demons and how to cast them out would come up. He encouraged me to read up on the subject.

People kept telling me that I should go to Tulsa, Oklahoma, the buckle of the Bible Belt. During the early 1980s, it was the boom city of evangelicals. New ministries would pop up overnight. Empty buildings suddenly would be transformed into a church with the new hot messenger of God. A few weeks later, the doors would be locked and the now cold messenger was nowhere to be found.

You could go to church almost 24 hours a day and some traveling pastor would be preaching somewhere in town. Some people even played a game of how many services they could attend in a day.

Sunday was the big day as the TV preachers videotaped their services and it was always the best service of the week.

I was learning but something didn't feel right. The messages were of the "name it and claim it" school of thinking. If you're a person of God you better be rich. If not, you're not of God. That went along with the message of healing but that healing came with the message of the law. There was little mentioned about the Cross, the Blood of Jesus, and nothing of grace.

I started to get to know some of the better preachers, but the more I got to know them, the more I saw and heard things that troubled me. They often bragged about their income or what kind of car they drove. Some even discussed getting a jet if they got on the Trinity Broadcast Network or one of the other big religious channels. They bragged about the women they loved—usually not their wives, and people they hired. Hired? Sure, because people needed to be healed and they hired folks to come up and get healed and saved. Those hired hands often earned upwards of $1,000 per week to fake it. They would keep on doing it as long as people didn't recognize them. Women usually lasted longer if they had a good supply of wigs and were willing to lose and add a few pounds from time to time.

I was able to do some teaching, but never on a Sunday. Occasionally, I got a Bible study group here and there. One day, two well-known evangelists, Paul and Jan Crouch, the founders of TBN, overheard me leading a study group. They offered to hook me up with the right people. I was told that I'd get rich as long as I talked and taught their messages and played by their rules.

That marked the end of my Tulsa days. Unsure of where to turn, at some of the more liberal churches I attended I began to hear the term "New Age." Much of what they talked about sounded like the old age as I'd read about psychics, mediums, channelers, gurus, etc. many years ago. The whole new age was starting to explode so I figured that maybe I'd find a spiritual home.

I started to attend every conference I could and followed every new age teacher, no matter what was being taught. I learned about:

- Mediation/relaxation

- Channeling

- Mediumship

- Psychic readings

- Tarot and other forms of card readings

- Past life regression

- Numerology

- Angelology

- Tealeaf readings

- Clairvoyance

- Healing and the chakras

- Remote viewing

Those were some of the topics I did in depth studies on. I even got to know some of the big new age teachers and discovered they were far worse than the Christian teachers I followed. For them, it was all about money, fame, power, and sex. They were competitive. They lied so they appeared to be knowledgeable and successful. I was taught all the tricks -- but never could follow them.

Finally, I was told to go to Los Angeles. Out there, they loved psychics and any type of new age mumbo jumbo they could hear. You could be terrible but if you kept at it, you'd find a following and make a good living.

So I hopped on a bus out west and arrived in the City of Angels. After putting up an ad, I waited for the phone to ring.

When it did, I was surprised. None of the calls were from people wanting a reading or channeling appointment. Instead, I got things like:

"I have a new home and since we moved in things have been moving around at night."

"My wife started playing with a spirit board and now she's not herself. Can you help?"

I began to think, what the heck is this?

God returned, though He'd never left—just had been silent as I stumbled along. He said, "Stop all this reading stuff that's not your path. People can come to me, not you, for help. Get rid of all the new age things and burn them. Stop talking to spirits. In most cases, they aren't spirits but demons. Get back to the Bible. Everything you need is in there."

Well, to get God talking to you like that what can you say? Out went all my psychic stuff. Admittedly, the house felt better afterwards. Looking up all the Bible passages concerning demons and everything Lester Sumrall taught me, I put together my first exorcism kit. It contained Bibles, crosses, prayers, holy water, and holy oil. The rest, as is said, is history. Now, years later, I'm still helping people as best as I can.

In 2008, I joined MySpace, and a year later, I was on Facebook. I run one of the top rated paranormal blogs called Eye on the Paranormal.
http://eyeontheparanormal.blogspot.com/

The paranormal from a Christian point of view is covered. We also expose paranormal fakes and frauds such as fake demonologists, and fake paranormal programs. No matter what, we don't back down.

Every Wednesday evening I host my own two-hour long radio show on the God Discussion Network. http://www.goddiscussion.net/2013/02/05/meet-the-hosts-kirby-robinson-eye-on-the-paranormal/

Many psychics tend to think that rules don't apply to them as they are special. They tend to classify these gifts in the following ways:

• Some say it is a gift given only to a few

• Some say everyone has the gift and they can teach you how to be psychic

• Some say they talk to angels, spirit guides, dead

people, and even God

- Some say they can heal

- Some say they can see what your illnesses are

- Some say their gift is the same one spoken of in the Bible

But the issue is who says what is true and what is not? In fact, you'll often see this disclaimer on many websites: FOR ENTERTAINMENT PURPOSES ONLY.

Would you visit a doctor or a pastor who had that sign hanging over their office door? Doubtful.

They charge for their services and we aren't talking a few dollars; some charge $1000 and up. What happens if you act on what they tell you and it's not the truth? Or if it's a half-truth? Are you ever compensated? No, because many don't even have enough basic business sense to have a refund policy.

I know the games they play. I know the jargon, the words, and the actions they take part in. That's why I'm able to write this book. That's why I can tell you the facts about how this works, why I can expose all the tricks and games they play on you, bilking you out of your hard-earned money, planting the seeds of lies and delusions that will grow within you for years to come. Read more if you aren't part of the deluded lemmings that believe whatever they see on "reality" TV and read on the Internet.

By the time you finish reading this book you'll see the Long Island Medium in a different light. And that goes for every psychic, medium, guru or new ager you may encounter.

CHAPTER 2
WHY PSYCHICS ARE DANGEROUS

Before I got my own radio show, I'd done several radio interviews on various other shows. If you've ever heard me, I usually share the two things that I feel are the biggest mistakes I've made in my life.

1. That I didn't take the time to become an ordained minister [I'm not talking about one of those free or $5 "certificated" ones]

2. That I did psychic readings

Play all the word games you want. Change the name and call yourself a psychic adviser or a spiritual counselor. Anytime you start to advise someone, whether you charge or don't charge for your services, you're still playing the role of God in some manner.

God knows everything—past, present and future. He

knows everything you've done [and thought] in the past. He knows what's in your heart and mind right now. He knows what you're predisposed to do. When it comes to the future, He knows where you're headed. All this knowledge is 100% accurate. Find a psychic that can do that. Find a psychic that has never been wrong. You won't. Because God is flawless.

I know what some psychic devotees are thinking right now. What about doctors, lawyers, accountants, etc.? They make mistakes. Does that mean we should avoid them? Absolutely not. Doctors, lawyers, accountants, etc. make honest human mistakes. But a psychic claims they have something special, something unseen, and something from the other side.

Before we move on, let's look at the following definitions of medium, psychic, channeler, psychic-medium, and healer.

Medium ~ Someone who claims that by some means they can hear from those who have passed away and are now on the other side.

Psychic ~ Someone who claims that by some means they can see what's in the future.

Psychic/Medium ~ A person that performs a function of both a psychic and a medium. If a person states they have such a title it's like they're claiming to be the best of the best. They're not just a psychic. They're not just a medium. They're a hybrid because they can predict the future, as well as to channel dead spirits.

Channeler ~ Someone who claims that by some means a spirit from the past [and in some cases a spirit from another world] will share insight.

Healer ~ Because of some power they can lay on hands. Or they claim they can do long-distance healings over the phone or Internet.

Many of these definitions might seem simplistic to those who have either spent a lot of time in the new age or reading about the new age. Often you'll find authors trying to dress up the definitions with fancy terms like *higher vibrations* or *flow of intelligent energy*. What they don't tell the reader is that there is little, if any, validity behind such terms. Ask 100 different people in the psychic world how being a psychic, a medium, or both, work. You'll get answers that will leave your head spinning and wondering if there is any validity to those terms.

In reality there is one person that can do all of the above.

~ He is free

~ He is always there

~ No appointment is needed

~ You don't need to buy a ticket to see Him in person. You don't have to watch him on TV. Nor do you have to buy a DVD to see Him.

He is God. You never hear *for entertainment purposes only*. No refunds, not responsible...those are things you don't read or hear about God.

What if you're not a Christian? Do you think that excludes you from His ways? I'm Jewish, I'm Muslim, I'm Hindu ... fine show me anyplace in their teachings where it says it's alright to contact spirits for information or help.

Buddhists are an exception to this as they have the Nechung Oracle who is actually considered a medium. He is a highly trained monk who is officially recognized as a State Oracle and continues a tradition that was established in the 8th century. Please note that there is only one. You can read more here: http://nechung.org/oracle/about.php.

Unlike Christians, Hindus and Buddhists believe in reincarnation. That shakes the foundation of many claims made by mediums and psychics. During a group or personal reading, have you ever heard a so-called gifted one say the following:

"I can't reach your mother due to the fact that she died x number of years ago and has gone through rebirth. Her mindstream has lost all traces of her past life except for the karmic debts she is carrying to her next life." You would hear this from a Buddhist, as the time in the bardo is very limited—it doesn't last for years or decades but usually only for a few weeks or months.

Or imagine hearing this:

"I can't reach your brother as he is not in the spiritual realm but has been reborn again as a boy. You can find him at xxx New Depot Street in Echo Park." Reincarnation in many Hindu and other Eastern belief paths is fixed so if you find that reincarnation, you find your lost brother.

In the Mahayana school of Buddhism, practitioners believe that there are six levels of samsaric existence ranging from rebirth in the highest God realms to the lowest hell realms. Therefore, a convincing example would be:

"I can't reach your favorite cousin as in his past life he was cruel to animals and so in his next life he lost his precious human rebirth and is living as a farm horse."

The Christian viewpoint is: "Your husband is living in heaven and due to his faith in the power of the Cross and Christ being his Savior he walked through the gates as pure as snow. Your husband was faithful with tithes to the church and his role in it, now he lives in a heavenly mansion."

I could go on and on. All you hear from these so-called returning spirits is the same new age view of the afterlife. The spirits repeat the same pat story of going into a white light once the storyteller dies. They meet loving family members and friends or maybe a helpful angel or spirit guide that will take them on an amazing cosmic journey. One such tale I recall was how the storyteller recounted sitting on a park bench outside the gates of heaven and an angel brought them a plate of fresh fruit that they claim had the most amazing taste ever! Once they did get into heaven, the first angel they encountered was a practical joker who did nothing but tell silly jokes. Other stories that you can hear or read about consist of flying across the universe and encountering alien cultures. It now seems popular to write books about such journeys but you never read about interacting with Jesus Christ and finding out whether the soul or the spirit is going to be allowed into heaven or found wanting and sent to hell. Because that wouldn't help attract readers/followers who would think, we better not see that medium because he or she might tell us that our criminal uncle or sister is burning in hell.

Either the teachings of God are true or not.

What mediums try to be [and they'll deny this] is many roles to the public. Why are they so multi-faceted? How else can they gain people's trust, take their money, and otherwise delude them? They claim to have information that you need. Then they board a plane and go back to their expensive homes. Or they spend your hard-earned money renovating their bathroom. Every day they increase their bank account[s], while emptying the bank accounts of their followers.

Worst of all, they lie.

They want to be your counselor, yet they have no training. They want to give you a false sense of hope so you can follow them [and not just on Facebook and Twitter]. They want to sell you their books, DVDs, readings, and make sure you convert your friends and family to become their followers. Then, when you find out that you've been lied to, they won't be around to blame. Or you'll feel that you've been so foolish that you remain silent.

While all the time there is someone you could turn to.

Let's take a look at what the Bible says about consulting psychics and mediums in both the Old and the New Testaments.

THE OLD TESTAMENT

Leviticus 19:31
"Do not turn to mediums or necromancers; do not

seek them out, and so make yourselves unclean by them: I am the Lord your God." ESV

This is very clear and easy to follow. Don't talk to or consult them, as by doing so you become unclean. Some people might say well, I'm saved, so God forgives me. Such thinking falls into tempting God's wrath.

Leviticus 20:6
"If a person turns to mediums and necromancers, whoring after them, I will set my face against that person and will cut him off from among his people." ESV

The term whoring is defined as a person who compromises their principles for personal gain. That gain doesn't mean wealth, it's for personal satisfaction. All the time you spend with them could be devoted to reading the Word of God, studying, and meditating with God. All the money you give psychics and such could have gone to God and the needs of the world.

Leviticus 20:27
"A man or a woman who is a medium or a necromancer shall surely be put to death. They shall be stoned with stones; their blood shall be upon them." ESV

Under the law of the Old Testament, stoning was a common practice [the laws of the Old Testament are harsh due to the sins of the Adam and Eve].

Deuteronomy 18:10-12
"There shall not be found among you anyone who burns his son or his daughter as an offering, anyone

who practices divination or tells fortunes or interprets omens, or a sorcerer or a charmer or a medium or a necromancer or one who inquires of the dead, for whoever does these things is an abomination to the Lord. And because of these abominations the Lord your God is driving them out before you." ESV

Very clear.

2 Chronicles 33:6
"And he burned his sons as an offering in the Valley of the Son of Hinnom, and used fortune-telling and omens and sorcery, and dealt with mediums and with necromancers. He did much evil in the sight of the Lord, provoking him to anger." ESV

This shows how partaking of such dark things opens our spirit to engage in even worse sins.

Exodus 7:10-12
"So Moses and Aaron went to Pharaoh and did just as the Lord commanded. Aaron cast down his staff before Pharaoh and his servants, and it became a serpent. Then Pharaoh summoned the wise men and the sorcerers, and they, the magicians of Egypt, also did the same by their secret arts. For each man cast down his staff, and they became serpents. But Aaron's staff swallowed up their staffs." ESV

This shows that Lucifer can copy the work of God. However, the copy isn't greater than the original. Why turn to someone who claims they know the future like God?

Isaiah 8:19-20
"And when they say to you, "Inquire of the mediums and the necromancers who chirp and mutter," should not a people inquire of their God? Should they inquire of the dead on behalf of the living? To the teaching and to the testimony! If they will not speak according to this word, it is because they have no dawn." ESV

People should turn to God instead of so-called seers.

Exodus 22:18
"You shall not permit a sorceress to live." ESV

The Old Testament was ruled by the law and the law was a terrible master. You had to live up to it and maintain it. There was no falling short. The punishment for such acts was being put to death. Once Christ came and died the law was fulfilled, so no actual death is called for. What will become of the person who takes part in it? It's a spiritual death as the person thinks they are a god or God. When they die, even though they may have fulfilled the requirements to reach heaven they've done so under a state of delusion and they'll find that they've been serving a dark master.

Leviticus 19:26
"You shall not eat any flesh with the blood in it. You shall not interpret omens or tell fortunes." ESV

A person can't interpret omens. Oftentimes mediums claim they don't talk to the spirits but they see things [omens], and they interpret them.

2 Kings 17:16-17

"And they abandoned all the commandments of the Lord their God, and made for themselves metal images of two calves; and they made an Asherah and worshiped all the host of heaven and served Baal. And they burned their sons and their daughters as offerings and used divination and omens and sold themselves to do evil in the sight of the Lord, provoking him to anger?" ESV

When we turn to other gods, even when we take a new god like Baal [who is a demon] then we replace prayer and meditation on the Word of God with other things like interpreting omens and talking to spirits [demons].

1 Chronicles 10:13-14
"So Saul died for his breach of faith. He broke faith with the Lord in that he did not keep the command of the Lord, and also consulted a medium, seeking guidance. He did not seek guidance from the Lord. Therefore the Lord put him to death and turned the kingdom over to David the son of Jesse." ESV

Talking to psychics and mediums can lead to God removing all He has given to your house and place it in the house of one who follows His Word.

2 Kings 9:22
"And when Joram saw Jehu, he said, "Is it peace, Jehu?" He answered, "What peace can there be, so long as the whorings and the sorceries of your mother Jezebel are so many?" ESV

We'll talk about the Jezebel spirit/demon later. The point of this passage states that peace [not necessarily talking about a time of external war] but a time of peace inside the nation, that isn't in a state of turmoil but of harmony. We can look at America and see turmoil and upheaval.

Darkness at the Edge of Town is a paranormal radio show hosted by Dave Schrader, a fan of psychics, mediums, and practitioners of the dark arts. One of his guests was psychic-medium Chip Coffey. Most of the interview was spent rewriting the Old Testament passages concerning psychic-mediums from the viewpoint that these rules don't apply today. They claimed that God changes as mankind changes. The host asked Mr. Coffey if there were any passages in the New Testament that warned people to stay away from such practices. "No!" Mr. Coffey stated, "There are none."

This statement gave the listener the idea that it's okay to talk to the dead and consult with psychics. In reality, there are many warnings against doing so that are found in the New Testament.

THE NEW TESTAMENT

1 John 4:1
"Beloved, do not believe every spirit, but test the spirits to see whether they are from God, for many false prophets have gone out into the world." ASV

We're warned to test test test the spirits and that false prophets are out there seeking victims to lead to hell.

Matthew 7:15
"Beware of false prophets, who come to you in

sheep's clothing but inwardly are ravenous wolves." ESV

These people come across as kindly, caring, and concerned but they aren't. They're all too happy to deceive the innocent.

Galatians 5 ;19-20
"Now the works of the flesh are evident: sexual immorality, impurity, sensuality, idolatry, sorcery, enmity, strife, jealousy, fits of anger, rivalries, dissensions, divisions, envy, drunkenness, orgies, and things like these. I warn you, as I warned you before, that those who do such things will not inherit the kingdom of God." ESV

When psychics/mediums push the viewpoint that if it feels good do it, you run into a huge problem. Because they also promote the myth of no sin, and no fear of a judgment when we die. Happiness and peace doesn't follow this teaching--what follows is a fast descent into sinning.

Acts 19: 17-19
"And this became known to all the residents of Ephesus, both Jews and Greeks. And fear fell upon them all, and the name of the Lord Jesus was extolled. Also many of those who were now believers came, confessing and divulging their practices. And a number of those who had practiced magic arts brought their books together and burned them in the sight of all. And they counted the value of them and found it came to fifty thousand pieces of silver." ESV

Magic arts = new age teaching

Acts 8: 9-13

"But there was a man named Simon, who had previously practiced magic in the city and amazed the people of Samaria, saying that he himself was somebody great. They all paid attention to him, from the least to the greatest, saying, "This man is the power of God that is called Great." And they paid attention to him because for a long time he had amazed them with his magic. But when they believed Philip as he preached good news about the kingdom of God and the name of Jesus Christ, they were baptized, both men and women. Even Simon himself believed, and after being baptized he continued with Philip. And seeing signs and great miracles performed, he was amazed." ESV

Simon was a great worker of the dark arts who was saved and turned to God when he saw the true power of God, and not the false power of Lucifer.

Acts 16:16-19

"As we were going to the place of prayer, we were met by a slave girl who had a spirit of divination and brought her owners much gain by fortune-telling. She followed Paul and us, crying out, "These men are servants of the Most High God, who proclaim to you the way of salvation." And this she kept doing for many days. Paul, having become greatly annoyed, turned and said to the spirit, "I command you in the name of Jesus Christ to come out of her." And it came out that very hour. But when her owners saw that their hope of gain was gone, they seized Paul and Silas and dragged them into the marketplace before the rulers." ESV

Here is a true appearance of SPIRIT. Something

allowed the young girl to contact multiple spirits so that she knew the good and the bad. She didn't know that it was a demon but was able to know who Paul was.

John 14:16
"But the Helper, the Holy Spirit, whom the Father will send in my name, he will teach you all things and bring to your remembrance all that I have said to you." ESV

You only need to reach out to the Holy Spirit to know all you need to know.

Revelation 21:8
"But as for the cowardly, the faithless, the detestable, as for murderers, the sexually immoral, sorcerers, idolaters, and all liars, their portion will be in the lake that burns with fire and sulfur, which is the second death." ESV

We all face physical death. No one gets out alive.

Revelation 22:15
"Outside are the dogs and sorcerers and the sexually immoral and murderers and idolaters, and everyone who loves and practices falsehood." ESV

Not only will this affect those that do, it will affect those who follow these teachers.

2 Thessalonians 2:9
"The coming of the lawless one is by the activity of Satan with all power and false signs and wonders."

ESV

Those who claim to be psychic-mediums are laying the foundation for the antichrist to come and make his false claims. They are helping to gather followers for him as their acts will be the antichrist's acts.

Revelation 16:14
"For they are demonic spirits, performing signs, who go abroad to the kings of the whole world, to assemble them for battle on the great day of God the Almighty. ESV

They seek to use the psychic-medium to fool all nations.

It's very clear that God doesn't endorse the psychic-medium. Have you ever heard any of those communications glorifying God? No, they always glorify the psychic-medium.

Theresa Caputo always states in her appearances and prior to her readings on the show that she doesn't care if you think her readings are legitimate. Why is this? Her followers would say it's because she is so sure, she KNOWS she's the real deal. I'd say it's due to the fact that if you doubt the spirits she works with they have no power over you. Her readings are very limited. You get three results.

1. Your departed loved one is with you.

2. They are okay.

3. Move on with your life.

No real predictions. No future events. Why doesn't she explain how her gift works? She claims she doesn't understand it, yet countless times she talks of seeing symbols like chocolate around the mouth meaning one thing and a light switch meaning another. Someone had to teach her this. She had to learn the process so she has an understanding. If she doesn't give her doubters anything to work with, then she controls the debate and doesn't have to defend herself. That way, she can claim a 100% accuracy rate.

Psychics and mediums, including those affiliated with the spiritualist church, know about the passages I've pointed out. What many have done is put on the cloak of prophet claiming that their gift is from God and they claim to glorify Him.

Let's take a look at what the Bible has to say about prophets:

1. Deuteronomy 18:21-22, "And if thou say in thine heart, How shall we know the word which Did the LORD hath not spoken? When a prophet speaketh in the name of the LORD, if the thing follow not, nor come to pass, that is the thing which the LORD hath not spoken, but the prophet hath spoken it presumptuously: thou shalt not be afraid of him." KJV

If a psychic-medium claims that his or her gift is from GOD, then every event that he/she says will happen must happen. This is the 100/100 rule. 100% of what they say will take place 100% of the time. The moment that it doesn't then the person isn't a prophet nor does their gift come from God.

2. Deuteronomy 18:21-22, "And if thou say in thine

heart, How shall we know the word which the LORD hath not spoken? When a prophet speaketh in the name of the LORD, if the thing follow not, nor come to pass, that is the thing which the LORD hath not spoken, but the prophet hath spoken it presumptuously: thou shalt not be afraid of him." KJV

True prophets will claim that they have dreams/visions that come from God. If they claim it comes from someone other than God they aren't a prophet.

3. Numbers 24:4 "He hath said, which heard the words of God, which saw the vision of the Almighty, falling into a trance, but having his eyes open:" KJV

Numbers 24:16, "He hath said, which heard the words of God, and knew the knowledge of the most High, which saw the vision of the Almighty, falling into a trance, but having his eyes open:" KJV

When they get a vision from God, their eyes must be open. If they aren't, they're not a prophet.

4. Daniel 10:17, "For how can the servant of this my lord talk with this my lord? For as for me, straightway there remained no strength in me, neither is there breath left in me." KJV

When they are communicating with God, they won't be breathing. If they claim they got a vision while still breathing, that means it doesn't come from God.

5. Daniel 10:17, "For how can the servant of this my lord talk with this my lord? for as for me, straightway

there remained no strength in me, neither is their breath left in me." KJV

The true prophet will fall to the ground as all the energy is sapped from them.

6. Daniel 10:18, "Then there came again and touched me one like the appearance of a man, and he strengthened me," KJV

The power of God will return the prophet to physical strength.

7. Jeremiah 28:9, "The prophet which prophesieth of peace, when the word of the prophet shall come to pass, then shall the prophet be known, that the LORD hath truly sent him." KJV

This is that 100% rule.

8. 2 Peter 1:20, "Knowing this first, that no prophecy of the scripture is of any private interpretation." KJV

When they share the Word, they are not to interpret the Lord only share the passage directly.

9. 2 Peter 1:21, "For the prophecy came not in old time by the will of man: but holy men of God spake as they were moved by the Holy Ghost." KJV

Their work is to glorify God -- not themselves.

10. 1 Corinthians 14:3-4, "But he that prophesieth speaketh unto men to edification, and exhortation, and comfort. He that speaketh in an unknown tongue edifieth himself; but he that prophesieth edifieth the church." KJV

A true prophet will, through his or her work, uplift the church, uplift the Word of God, and seek to glorify them but never seek personal glory.

11. Isaiah 8:20, "To the law and to the testimony: if they speak not according to this word, it is because there is no light in them." KJV

A true prophet will follow the Word fully and will follow the Ten Commandments. You WON'T see a true prophet kill, steal, lie, commit adultery, worship false idols, or disobey any of the Commandments. They won't be sinless, as there is only one sinless, but a true prophet will not be of or into worldly things.

12. 1 John 4:1-3, "Beloved, believe not every spirit, but try the spirits whether they are of God: because many false prophets are gone out into the world. Hereby know ye the Spirit of God: Every spirit that confesseth that Jesus Christ is come in the flesh is of God: And every spirit that confesseth not that Jesus Christ is come in the flesh is not of God: and this is that spirit of antichrist, whereof ye have heard that it should come; and even now already is it in the world." KJV

A true prophet seeks to bring glory to Jesus and His message of the Cross.

There are two types of prophets.

1] Prophets of God. They will be like Christ in the sense that their works bring forth good fruits. Their message uplifts and helps people, changing lives for the better, bringing them closer to God and an understanding of Him and His message.

2] Prophets of the antichrist. They produce everything opposite of the prophets of God. They don't see what is really going to happen 100% of the time. They might get some things right and that's just to trick people. Their goal is to bring people closer to the antichrist dressed up as Christ. At some point, the message will reveal itself.

Unless the prophet meets every one of the above 12 factors they aren't a prophet.

From the Catholic Catechism:

2115 God can reveal the future to his prophets or to other saints. Still, a sound Christian attitude consists in putting oneself confidently into the hands of Providence for whatever concerns the future, and giving up all unhealthy curiosity about it. Improvidence, however, can constitute a lack of responsibility.

2116 All forms of divination are to be rejected: recourse to Satan or demons, conjuring up the dead or other practices falsely supposed to "unveil" the future. Consulting horoscopes, astrology, palm reading, interpretation of omens and lots, the phenomena of clairvoyance, and recourse to mediums all conceal a desire for power over time, history, and, in the last analysis, other human beings, as well as a wish to conciliate hidden powers. They contradict the honor, respect, and loving fear that we owe to God alone.

Are people helped? Are they saved? Does their faith in the Word of God grow? Now ask yourself if you've you seen this take place after watching any of these psychics or psychic-mediums? Have you observed this with the Long Island Medium? The only thing I've ever noticed is that prior to a reading, she looks like she's biting her tongue or cheek. [More on this later].

Additionally you'll find nothing about pay. Yes, prophets were paid. People brought them food, small gifts, money, and some offered them shelter. Prophets are human beings and they have needs, but they aren't high maintenance. They don't need black marble bathrooms and luxury automobiles.

Go to a psychic-medium and offer a dozen apples, or some wine. Offer a place to stay for the night. Now see how many readings you'll get. Go to one of these psychics and tell them you have no money but need a reading and see what you get.

Lastly, if a Christian pastor would say he wants you to pay him $200 to talk to God, imagine the outcry you'd hear over that.

My final point on this subject is that when you visit a psychic-medium and pay for their service, you're committing spiritual prostitution. When you visit God, you get a true relationship.

The psychic/medium/channeler/healer charges you for their "help."

God offers His help for free.

The psychic/medium/channeler/healer says they care about you.

God cares so much he sent His Son to die for you.

You'll wait days/weeks/months or even years to see a psychic/medium/channeler/healer.

God is there for you 24/7.

The psychic/medium/channeler/healer says this is for entertainment purposes only.

God says this is for eternity purposes.

The psychic/medium/channeler/healer says there are subjects off limits.

There is nothing off limits with God.

The psychic/medium/channeler/healer says I can't diagnose you for health issues.

God says I know everything about you and your body.

The psychic/medium/channeler/healer can't heal you.

God can.

The psychic/medium/channeler/healer can only guess about the afterlife.

God created the afterlife so He knows everything about it.

The psychic/medium/channeler/healer is gone at

the end of the reading.

God always stays by your side.

The psychic/medium/channeler/healer loves your money.

God Loves YOU!

So ... I think you get my point.

Some might say that you can't compare readers to prostitutes due to the fact that prostitution has far more crime connected to it. But that even fails to pass the logic test.

~ In most places charging for a reading is illegal.

~ Storefront psychics and/or Internet psychics con people out of money. Oftentimes they claim they can break curses or remove hexes when they can't.

~ Some claim to be able to heal and charge for this--which is illegal.

~ Some involved in the psychic field don't always report their earnings to the IRS.

~ Those engaging in past life therapy are unaccredited. No state will license this type of therapy.

~ They commit fraud as they claim that they can teach people to be a psychic/medium/channeler/healer, yet they're unable to do any of the above.

Yes, consulting a psychic is like spiritual prostitution.

CHAPTER 3
TRYING TO MAKE SENSE OF PSYCHIC NONSENSE

They aren't even sure of what's going on

There is one more topic we'll cover prior to unearthing the truth behind the amazing readings given by the Long Island Medium. We need to come to an understanding of what psychics and mediums claim to do and how they do it.

First, let me say this, and I hope this doesn't seem as if it's a blanket condemnation of all psychics and psychic-mediums. There are some good yet misguided people in the field. Not all of them are blinded by fame, money, and power. Not all of them have a hidden spiritual agenda. Some feel for the hurting and for those who come to them for a reading. Yet that desire is rooted in an area it shouldn't be due to the fact that they are just doing as they have been taught. They have been misguided into believing that this is the way things should be done.

When we talk about psychic-mediums some will tell you it's a gift that through past lives here on earth, or on other planets, and even lives lived in the spirit realm, have prepared them to do this. Another explanation is that some higher order of beings in the spirit world has sent them to impart knowledge and wisdom. They are special, they are above others. There is only one of them. They have been seduced by whatever "spiritual entity" they have come into contact with. Or is this their ego running rampant? Often, they will have lived lives in which they have even been put to death or tortured to prepare them for now.

Some psychics will say that the ability to see and hear from the spiritual realm has come to them suddenly -- the gift just magically appears. I'm not sure that all the classes, seminars and books that I've ever read on the subject ever added anything additional to the gift, like making it stronger, clearer, etc.

Other psychics will claim they learned to be a psychic by taking classes or reading books. The student gives permission to a spirit being that is often called a spirit guide/angel. That entity "belongs" to some teacher. Oftentimes the spirit is labeled as a superior being, an elder, an ancient one, or even a god.

Injuries, accidents, and even NDE's [Near Death Experiences] have led some to being a psychic and opened doors to the spirit realm.

A psychic always claims at some point to find a teacher. That teacher will show them the way. In the case of Theresa Caputo, that teacher was Pat Longo.

The student is definitely a chip off the old block.

http://patlongo.net/

Her site sheds light on why Theresa does her readings the way she does. Her new age mindset comes from Pat, who had a great influence on Theresa's view of the spiritual realm.

The website proclaims that this is Gifted Spiritual Healer Pat Longo

There is little doubt of what the visitor is going to learn while they visit the page. In headline font, we see a snippet of a famous Bible passage:

"...AND TO SOME GOD GAVE THE GIFT OF HEALING"

The full passage reads:

1 Corinthians 12:28
"And God hath set some in the church, first apostles, secondarily prophets, thirdly teachers, after that miracles, then gifts of healings, helps, governments, diversities of tongues." KJV

What this passage is talking about is that of THE CHURCH. It doesn't refer to every group out there or to every single person. Here are the five important elements.

1. Apostles. Those are people who spread the message of the Cross -- not a new age message.

2. Prophets. They deliver news to followers and non-followers of things to come, how to avoid them, and what will happen if you don't. Prophets never do

personal readings.

3. Teachers are there to help us understand the Message of the Cross.

4. Workers of Miracles show that they serve the most high God. Those serving lesser gods are never able to perform all the deeds of the true miracle worker.

5. Healers are people who simply open up their body and channel the healing energies of God. It's not necessary for God to operate through a healer as in the cases of the miraculous healings performed by Christ, particularly the Centurion's servant that was healed by Christ as He said he was healed. God can rain down His healing power and not go through a person. But it can be a tool of recruitment for the lost/unsaved to see a person operating under the power of God, laying of hands, and healing.

What new agers fail to understand is that the above five elements aren't meant to bring glory to oneself but to God. Nowhere will you read anything about charging for these services.

On Pat's site we see this paragraph.

*I **have** been an energy healer and spiritual teacher for the past 20 years. **I, myself,** was taking a spiritual awareness class when **I** was blessed with **my** gift of healing. **I have** helped countless men, women and children overcome various illnesses, anxieties and emotional traumas.*

Pat claims that for 20 years she has healed [amazingly enough Pat takes credit for the healing]. How does she work these healings? By getting on her knees in prayer? By pleading to God by the Blood of Jesus? By claiming that Christ died so we may be healed? No, she says something about some bright light that flows through her.

2 Corinthians 11:14
"And no marvel; for Satan himself is transformed into an angel of light." KJV

Because Pat writes on her front page that what "she channels through her body is from pure light and love" doesn't make it so.

She claims that she's responsible for healings. In the above referenced 46-word paragraph she uses the word I four times, and my and myself once each. Also, she claims four levels of healing!

- Physical

- Mental

- Emotional

- Spiritual

Now let's stop and reflect on the enormity of such an all-encompassing claim. There is only one other person that can help people be healed on all four levels like that--Jesus Christ.

Notice there isn't any type of disclaimer on the page. Nor do we see any percentages listed of successes and failures. By default, that means she boasts a 100% success rate.

You don't have to travel to her home to get a healing as she can do one over the phone. When Christ healed the young servant of a centurion, He didn't have a phone, He just told him the boy was healed. Christ never charged a cent, nor did any of His followers. Pat feels a need to charge not ten bucks, or fifty, but $175 for a healing.

In the state of New York, it's illegal for someone claiming to possess occult powers to charge for them. Why hasn't the state not stepped in? What about the American Medical Association or the American Psychological Association? Nowhere on her website does Pat claim to have medical training.

http://law.onecle.com/new-york/penal/PENO165.35_165.35.html

§ 165.35 Fortune telling. "A person is guilty of fortune telling when, for a fee or compensation which he directly or indirectly solicits or receives, he claims or pretends to tell fortunes, or **holds himself out as being able, by claimed or pretended use of occult powers, to answer questions or give advice on personal matters or to exorcise, influence or affect evil spirits or curses**; except that this section does not apply to a person who engages in the aforedescribed conduct as part of a show or exhibition solely for the purpose of entertainment or amusement. Fortune telling is a class B misdemeanor."

"Class B misdemeanor. A sentence to pay a fine for a class B misdemeanor shall be a sentence to pay an amount, fixed by the court, not exceeding five hundred dollars."

I can hear the new age singers getting ready for the tune of what's the difference between a Christian pastor who lays on hands and Pat Longo who does healings in person or over the phone? Well for one, no Christian pastor will charge money for it or there will be many people and organizations, including myself, that will come after him. Secondly, they must advise that medical help shouldn't be abandoned.

Pat also teaches a class and shows you how to heal yourself. Now that student can also charge $175 for a healing.

Let's do some math.

1 = $175.00

10 = $1,175.00

100 = $17,500.00

1000 = $175,000.00

Healing sure pays well!

If you keep digging, you'll find even more interesting information.

- Her bio is very similar to Theresa's.

- Unlike Theresa Caputo, who claims she was born with the gift, Pat claims she was taking a self-awareness class and it worked so well she began to heal men, women, and children of all forms of illnesses.

- There is a short blog about healing and how people get sick.

"Learn to heal your life by going within and learning forgiveness of self and others. Illness begins to manifest itself by the thoughts that you have of hurt, anger, loss, and fear, etc. It starts with the thought first, then the emotion and if the emotion is held onto for too long, it will then manifest itself into the physical body as an illness."

A few years ago, Pat Longo had a bout with cancer even going through surgery to become cancer free. Her husband Vincent died on August 18, 2012 from cancer. So we have to ask why did the two not go through healing sessions from others to avoid surgery and death altogether? How can she heal if she herself is partaking in such thinking that produces illness in both her and her late husband?

She used to teach a spiritual awareness class. In June 2013, she passed on the responsibility to others. However, she has hosted workshops on such topics:

Learning how to manifest

What are we supposed to manifest?

Instruction in Automatic Writing

Any type of class that opens you up to automatic writing is allowing spirits into your body. Spirits are not angels from heaven or kindly spirit guides but demonic entities and demons.

Mediumship Workshops

Pat is in the camp of believing and teaching that it's not really a gift but the ability that everyone has. This is how you open yourself to demonic attacks.

Healing Workshops

The demonic can copy everything good that God can do. Such classes allow the demonic to seduce the public into the false miracles from Lucifer.

On Pat's contact page she also claims to do:

- Chakra awareness and balancing
- House clearings and blessings

Chakras are simply the balance points within the body that the new agers have hijacked from common sense.

As to house clearings/cleansings and blessings, we see more and more of this. It requires people to run throughout a home with a lit stick or bundle of sage. Saging [sometimes referred to as smudging] doesn't drive out the demonic. It doesn't do anything other than smell an area up for a few minutes. It's also an easy payday. Blessing a home in the name of Christ is the most effective way for Christians.

Saging is very popular within the new age and with so-called lightworkers. They walk around a room, home, building, even property holding a seashell full of burning sage. They use a feather to help fan out the smoke. [It can't be an eagle feather as both bald and golden eagles are protected by law, and only those with a permit can legally obtain them.] Some kind of prayer is said, oftentimes addressing god/goddess/all angels/all spirit guides/love and light. Some kind of prayer and/or chant is done and that's supposed to drive out spirits.

Both Pat and Theresa do this. Not sure who taught who about it, and that's not important. What the reader needs to know is that this kind of stuff is worthless for the most part. If you are a Christian, you won't find any chapter or verse in the Bible that mentions it. It won't remove evil spirits or demons. There is nothing mystical about sage, it's just an herb.

The new age highjacked this from Native Americans because it looks cool but it doesn't make it real.

Claims that it's the real deal are just that ... claims. It's like the placebo effect just because you do it you feel better, your home feels better, but it's not.

If demons and evil spirits that we encounter responded to simple smoke, then many people's work would be far easier. But that's how the spiritual darkness works. It convinces you to turn from the Word.

Back to Pat's website.

• Pat is eager to push the *Long Island Medium* show since she has appeared on it twice so far. [We'll look into her second appearance shortly]. She is happy to provide a link to Amazon so you can buy single episodes or the whole season.

• Pat selflessly provides a self-guided meditation for free. What she doesn't warn you is that often people taking part in this find themselves under demonic attack.

• Her links page is simply a list to other psychic/mediums in the New York City/Long Island area, which shouldn't be surprising. Further digging unleashes interesting information.

The first is a link to Theresa Caputo's website.

Sandy Ricciardi's link no longer works.

Kim Russo a/k/a The Happy Medium, is a big fan of paranormal reality TV. Long before Theresa Caputo shot her pilot, Kim appeared on A&E's *Paranormal State* in the second season. According to Kim's website, it appears she played a far larger role in it than her one episode. She was hired to appear in *Psychic Kids: Children of the Paranormal* a very controversial program that featured Chip Coffey and Chris Fleming overseeing two or three kids over the course of a weekend. Now these weren't ordinary kids, they were allegedly psychic kids. They never show how these kids are psychic outside of the children's [usually outlandish] claims. Also, the children oftentimes come from single parent homes, so the mother [tho' there are some single dads, too] declare their kids are special. After the show went off the air, some parents had their kids do psychic readings for a fee. One family is helping their son and daughter come up with a new religion. During the first season of *Psychic Kids*, two teenage girls were taken into a home that was supposedly filled with demons. After the show aired, one of the girls came under demonic attack and no one affiliated with the show helped in any way.

Kim currently is on a show called *The Haunting of* that features D-list celebrities talking about being haunted. This enables Kim to solve everything in one hour—minus commercials.

Laura Lynne Jackson is happy to charge you $450 for a 90-minute reading. She claims, along with Kim and Tracy, that the Forever Family Foundation has certified her. Laura also alleges that she sees a new spiritual awakening coming.

Bobbi Allison is the last link. This site seems to have one goal: to get you to buy a reading. Nothing else is seen on it.

Our tour through Pat Longo's page and our look at "her girls" proves much of what is said in the first part of the book. So let's begin to focus on the readings of the Long Island Medium and the truth behind her show.

CHAPTER 4
HAVE WE SEEN A REAL READING FROM THERESA?

The short answer is simple.

No.

The public has never seen a complete reading from her. The only people who have are those who paid for a private reading or received a one-on-one reading during an episode.

What rules are there? Notice that you never see anyone taking notes or using their own recording device, which are things I always encouraged when I did readings. Also, for someone earning upwards of $800 per hour, why does she use an obsolete cassette-recording tape recorder dating back to the 1970s?

Theresa's readings are like magic tricks. What you think you see is not really what happened.

Let's look at the readings you've seen on her show.

1. *Spontaneous Readings*

You know the ones she gives when she goes to a gas station, a park, a liquor store, grocery store, shoe store, ice skating rink, etc.

When a production company decides to shoot at any location, they can't go to the corner gas station and start filming because they want to. First, the production company must obtain filming permits not only from the clerk's office but also from the property/business owner. The production company must also provide an insurance certificate.

Here is a link to the laws within the state of New York.
http://www.resource411.com/pdf/FilmingNY_State.pdf

If you're just going to set up a camera and keep it running throughout your shoot at a particular site, you must post notices that if you enter, or are within range of a camera, you'll be filmed. We have never seen a Notice of Filming during an episode. Here is an example of one:
http://sonnyboo.com/downloads/noticeoffilming.pdf

Any individual Theresa interacts with on camera must sign a release form in order to be shown on TV. Therefore, the idea that Theresa just gets these messages at a spur of a moment is false.

Let me use a recent "instant" reading to demonstrate that, just like a magic trick, it's not an instant reading, it's a staged one.

In the *Why Me?* episode, Theresa stops at an Ultra

gas station to fill up the tank of her white SUV. The camera follows her as she goes inside the store/payment area and talks to the cashier. That cashier had to fill out a release form, agreeing that he could be filmed and later shown on TV. She returns to her vehicle and begins to fill up the gas tank. Then she does her instant reading preparation action. Whether this action is a signal, or whether it's conscious or not, you can observe it whenever she does one of these spontaneous readings. It involves smacking her lips and chewing on the inside of her cheek or tongue.

Theresa goes on to the other side of the gas pump and starts talking to a man in a black jacket named Freddie. The topic of conversation is his parents.

- Permission had to be granted to film at the gas station

- Cameras had to be set up to film

- Permission had to be give by Freddie in order to be filmed

- Gas stations located off major streets and highways are very busy. Do you hear anyone blowing a horn or yelling? Why is this? More than likely it's staged.

Why are we never given the first and last name of people she reads for? Does it look more authentic that she walks up to Freddie or Mary at some public location? On the show that we helped thoroughly debunk as fake, *Paranormal State*, we learned that they would pull people from the production crew to use as fake experts or witnesses to staged events. Not surprisingly, Magilla Productions also uses this tactic.

Why doesn't Theresa ever encounter an individual who doesn't want a reading? Or a person who is hostile to her and what she represents? Or someone who grudgingly allows her to read for them, only to have Theresa get things completely wrong? Undoubtedly, these things have happened but you'll never see them on TV.

In Chapter 8 when we deal with the Florida road trip she took in order to give readings to her adoring fans, we'll debunk it even more.

2. *Theresa Caputo Live: The Experience*

In the fall of 2012, Theresa launched a nationwide tour in order to do large readings in halls and theatres. While not in the league of filling Shea Stadium or the Hollywood Bowl, most of the venues seat approximately 2,000 to 3,000 people.

Now if she gets hits in the halls and theatres, she can really prove she is gifted -- correct? Not at all. We know of an internet psychic who does the same thing but on a much smaller scale. They begin to sell tickets several months before the event. Seating is assigned so they know where everyone will be sitting during the event.

If you ever buy a ticket for such an event notice the amount of information you reveal:

- Your name

- Street address

- Phone number [home/work or cell]

- Your age

- Email address

- Credit card information

- Names of others that are attending with you

- Sometimes the names of people you wish to reach and why

All of this information allows anyone to do a complete investigation into you and your family.

- Where you live [current and past addresses]

- Where you work [current and previous employment]

- Who are your parents? Are they alive or dead? If deceased, how did they die?

- Who are your children? Are they alive or dead? If deceased, how did they die?

- Have you suffered from any major illnesses?

Would they do this for everyone? No, of course not. But if you know where everyone will be seated, you can easily choose people from various sections. A good showman will select people no matter what they paid for their seats. So she'll read for people from the high priced seats in the front to those in the less expensive areas.

And if you find a real juicy story, that's always a way to enhance your talent. But doing this kind of a scam can backfire on you, which it did at a show in

Boston. Three thousand fans crammed themselves into every seat in the house at the Wang Theatre on April 12, 2013.

Theresa Caputo and *Spirit* were doing their little act when they came up to two women sitting in the theater. The Long Island Medium gave one woman a quick reading that could and would fit anyone in that audience. But a friend that came along with her had a far more interesting tale concerning a bad relationship with her dad who had passed on. Theresa claimed she was trying to reach out to the woman who was having none of it. She refused to listen and Theresa took the hint and moved on.

Temporarily. Theresa refused to let it go and returned; the woman again refused to listen and told the medium to leave her alone which she did. When Theresa bothered her for the third time, moments later, the irritated woman called her a fake and the star of the show had her removed by security.

Why would she keep going back to this woman unless it was such a great story? Out of the 3,000 audience members, Theresa can't give each person a reading. Plus, many people have similar stories. So what she now does is claim that if she gives a reading to one that it can apply to many in the audience. I'm sure that in life we have relationships with others that are unique to us and the other person. Such claims are self-serving for Theresa. Therefore, people can't get mad when they realize she only read for about twenty people rather than all of them. They paid the same amount of money as the person that got a direct reading from Theresa. Someone sitting in the back row who paid for it can say I lost my father and the woman who lost her father in the front row got a reading from Theresa. So back row woman should be happy that front row woman heard from her father. That should be enough. That should be fine [because Theresa only does fine].

This is a growing trend amongst psychics and mediums who are performing large and small events, public readings/gallery readings. People are duped into paying for a ticket and not being serviced. It's like going to a buffet and watching other people eat the best foods like large amounts of prime rib and lobster, and you get stuck with hot dogs and macaroni and cheese.

3. *Small Group Readings on the Show*

Theresa claims that all she knows about readings is the contact name and address of the site for the reading. This is probably true. But that would only apply to her and not the production company staff members.

Those affiliated with the production company would have to know about the site. They would go there to see how to film and what setup would be needed.

Permission would have to be granted to film there. Anyone attending the group reading would have to sign a release form. Production company employees and crewmembers get shots of people prior to the readings. They overhear people saying I want to hear from my late husband Bob or my daughter Sarah, and wow, they just happen to hear from that person.

4. *Personal Readings on the Show*

Just like the small group readings, the same can be

said for the one or two person readings Theresa does. Due to her enormous popularity [mostly attributed to her show], getting a reading from her can now take up to three years. You have to provide the same amount of information that you do when you order tickets. Additionally, the producers want very sad, painful readings for the sake of drama. Also, how many people send emails and letters asking for readings? That gives Theresa and her team information to build from.

The readings are edited so we really don't know what went on. It's done for the sake of the show's time limit, it's done for the sake of drama, as no one wants to watch Theresa staring off into space in order to get answers from *Spirit*. On the other hand, what if *Spirit* isn't batting a thousand that day or maybe is goofing with her and Theresa says "Uncle Richard liked young boys." Oops, the client was supposed to hear from Aunt Kate? As in most reality shows, they show the person/s featured in the reading talking to the camera and telling us what they expected from the reading. Was this filmed before or after the reading? To further dupe the viewers, we're oftentimes shown photos of the dearly departed. When did the production team get these photos?

But her most important readings are her TV appearances on talk shows where she does the cold reading shtick.

CHAPTER 5
THE SCIENCE OF COLD READINGS

Cold readings and all the little tricks behind them is what fuels 99.9% of all psychics and mediums especially if they're doing large readings. Incidentally, some of them even do these tricks during one-on-one readings.

But first—don't forget the plants!

~ Some psychics have such a loyal following they can get [hire] folks willing to sit in an audience and play a role for a psychic.

~ Other types of plants are those who join the audience prior to the filming of a show and get to know people who have interesting or entertaining stories. These gregarious plants will find out:

- Your name

- Are you a big fan of the psychic-medium?

- Some things about you – favorite food, your job, where you live, hobbies, etc.

- Details of who you want to hear from and why

This information is shared with the Cold Reader and either written down or relayed over a microphone or via hand signals from someone in the audience.

A cold reading is the process where the cold reader gets all the information they need or at least enough knowledge that'll let them fill in the details. Subsequently, this allows them to trick a person into thinking that they have information on them that only a psychic/medium could know. That makes them good at being able to fake things.

This is how it's done. The cold reader must possess the ability to ask many questions that are broad but can be narrowed down to specifics when necessary. The cold reader is usually an extravert. They have a very likable personality. They are self-assured, confident, stylish, and charismatic. The cold reader has the ability to distract the person being read, in carnival terms, the mark. Your average cold reader possesses a high EQ [emotional intelligence], coupled with the ability to appear empathetic to other people's emotions. In fact, the cold reader can appear quite the opposite when they become teary-eyed. Also, they take general information into account:

- Body language

- Age

- Gender

- Their dress code: business attire, sportswear, slutty, rocker, etc.?

- Religion – crosses, Star of David, prayer beads

- Race/ethnicity

- Sexual orientation

All of these points can help a reader fill in a complex and seemingly complete reading.

The larger the crowd the better. The odds are more in their favor as the cold reader can safely use more general questions.

For example, the cold reader might say:

~ Who on this side of the audience has lost a child or maybe a grandchild?

You know that's going to get reactions, allowing the cold reader to note those that respond. The cold reader might select a person to read. Or they might want to be more sure of selecting a mark that'll put on a good show.

~ I want to say this person was either a teenager or maybe a little younger.

~ Sometimes there's an eager participant. This person will blurt out information without realizing they are saying things. For example, "That's my grandson Bobby."

~ The cold reader now has a victim

I see a young man by the name of Billy ... pause ...

no ... Bobby. He liked out of door things [safe bet] then he/she will start shotgunning questions toward the person. This is where luck comes into play. The cold reader can ask things and get hits or misses. The lucky ones get yeses. If not, they break the reading off and go to a different part of the audience. However, we'll stick with the grandchild Bobby who passed away. Look at the mark's body language. Is Bobby's grandma shaking? Is she teary-eyed or already crying? Does she wear a wedding ring? All those signs give the cold reader openings to go deeper into the reading.

~ The cold reader will keep a list of assumptions about the person being read. Also, they'll notice the people near her. How are they reacting? Are they talking?

~ "My husband Dan died from cancer he left me too soon." That statement can give them information to use later when they flubbed a reading or start to miss too often.

The cold reader will keep eye contact going at all times. When people are looking at them, they don't have time to be thinking too much about the reading and what is said.

Once the cold reader has lowered the hook into the subject's mouth, they'll go from cold to warm and fuzzy. If the person cries, the cold reader will cry and even say the spirit is also crying. They'll reassure the subject that they must help them interpret the signs. Why? Because the information is a gift from beyond and they're just the channel.

The cold reader can make other attendees feel special. They'll say that even though they're reading this one person, that information is for others in the audience who have lost someone. [Theresa frequently uses this bit and even calls it piggybacking.] This keeps the entire audience from getting restless and makes them feel like they're part of the show. While a large percentage of the audience won't get a direct reading from the cold reader, they'll feel like they got a reading. This makes them feel like the cold reader is right 100% of the time.

~ Saints Sell! Notice how successful cold readers use powerful buzzwords like GOD, ANGELS, SPIRIT GUIDES, and HEAVEN in their exchange. It makes the audience feel like that cold reader is very spiritual and such a person can't be a fake.

~ Cold readers like to go fishing. If asking a question [this is where being lucky comes into play] and it's right, that just reaffirms their so-called ability.

~ Successful cold readers are positive. Note: this is the main key I use to find fake psychics, as they don't talk about hell, suffering, demons, etc. Why? Warm and fuzzy readings sell. People want to believe there are angels. Cold readers won't tell their clients that your dad says you were a lazy SOB or that you screwed up your life by marrying that jerk.

~ They use Barnum Statements. This term comes from the famous circus showman, P.T. Barnum. Barnum Statements are generalized statements that can apply to most people in the audience. The cold reader says things that anyone should know but they can make it seem personalized. Examples: "You loved your son/grandson." "You miss your husband." You can use phrases like "he told me this" or "he wants you to know he knew." More general statements: you're unhappy in your job, you're having problems with a friend or relative, you like watching movies.

~ People think that the biggest part of cold readings is to keep talking but that's not always true. Sometimes it's effective to stop and act like you are carrying on a conversation with the person that's in the spiritual realm because then people can say they're seeing a medium interact with a spirit!

~ One trick is the Rehash. The person being read says, "My departed daughter loved the color yellow." The cold reader will fire it right back at the person making others think they said it. They'll elaborate on that yellow by saying they see a girl bathed in yellow light and wearing a yellow dress and writing with a yellow pen on yellow stationary. The person will suddenly exclaim that her daughter used to have a pen with a yellow feather on it and that will send everyone in a tizzy of applause. This will confirm how great the cold reader is.

~ Cold Reader as Ringmaster. Another term originating from the circus. Ringmasters are the emcees, the ones who are in charge of the show. Cold readers are fantastic ringmasters. They are natural leaders and are very convincing. They also know when to break things up with laughter.

~ Cold readers are always right. For example, "I am never wrong these are the signs I see it's up to you to decide how it applies to you."

This is how cold readers operate. They have all the elements that can convince countless people into believing that they are psychics/mediums, and/or channelers.

However, to complete this chapter, let's ask who could do these kinds of things? Because honestly, they're just using people. They dish out false information, false hope, and false faith and simply leave them with a pile of lies.

CHAPTER 6
AN AUDIENCE READING FROM THERESA CAPUTO

Here is an audience reading performed by Theresa Caputo to show you the cold reading in action.

Live With Kelly and Michael ~ Friday, September 14, 2012

http://www.youtube.com/watch?v=OzxCkGxipyI

It's recommend that you read this section first, and then carefully watch the 8:54 clip. Things will come fast and furious—Mrs. Caputo has developed a rapid-fire delivery over the years. At times, she talks so quickly she almost sounds like an auctioneer.

Observe that as the segment starts she's not that comfortable. When she begins, she breaks the audience down into three groups and starts with the people seated at the right-hand side of the studio.

As she and Kelly walk over, she clears up the fact that she didn't get anything wrong earlier, she simply was confused.

Question 1 "Did somebody over here lose a husband? Who lost a husband?" See how she's repeating herself? Also, the loss of a husband [usually] affects a woman and if you're lucky, someone that will cry. She then says how sorry she was—showing her humanity and concern for the widow wearing a black sweatshirt.

Question 2 "Was your husband ill prior to his passing?" Theresa claims that you can leave this world in many different ways. False. Unless he died in an accident, he died from an illness.

Notice how Theresa talks up the care the widow gave to her husband making her feel very good. She adds that her husband might not have been the easiest person to take care of [she's pretending to have a conversation with the dead person. This makes her look very gifted and she inserts laughter]. Also, note how the unnamed dead husband "is funny" and Theresa laughs. Theresa reports that the deceased man said, "Well I can be a bit stubborn, Theresa." Yet the widow's name isn't mentioned, nor is that of the departed man.

Question 3 When discussing something the departed man ate, she gets a negative reaction from the widow in the black sweatshirt. In order to cover her error, Theresa says, "My meaning is signs and symbols—it doesn't mean that they're incorrect it means that it might just have a different meaning for you." Then she uses the myth that the "spirits" eat on the other side. How illogical!

What type of food can a spirit eat? Do they dine at an ethereal replica of their favorite restaurant? Do they shop at a supermarket and then cook food in their ethereal kitchen? How can a spirit eat something physical? When you see a reader inserting such myths you know you're dealing with a ringmaster.

Theresa's played out here and decides it's time to move onto a new person.

Question 4 is classic -- has someone lost a loved one? She might as well ask if everyone in the audience is alive.

Question 5 "Now I want to talk about who's wearing the picture of someone." She's patting her throat, physically selling the concept. "It's like a bunch of charms ... or like a bunch of articles wearing around your neck." Notice how she says that they have to be "from people that have departed."

She focuses on a woman in the front row wearing a pale pink shirt with a white blouse worn over it.

Question 6 "Is your mom passed?" The woman in white clearly shakes her head no. Theresa fails to connect with that response, as the next few comments seem to be as if Theresa is acting as if she is talking to a non-dead person. She flounders around until she finds a woman in the front row wearing a white crocheted top. Theresa uses her abilities and laughter to trick the audience and validates the woman by mentioning an engagement ring. But she goes broader with that asking if the woman has the ring, changed the ring or given it to someone else. [Usually the ring goes to the daughter or maybe the only child].

Question 7 "Now whose brother died--or brother-in-law?" Only one woman appears to hold her hand up in that section and a few others seem hesitant. Uh oh, that's not good. She quickly picks a mark—that of a woman, wearing a beige sweater, who raises her hand. Also, a woman in a dark pink top, sitting next to her, points her out. Theresa teaches the audience more of her shtick by revealing that: "I like spirits that piggyback, okay? 'Cause what happens if even I say something and I never look in your direction but something is said that you can connect with and place in your life or that of your loved one or connect with your loved ones please accept as a message from him. It happens all the time. *Spirit* has me say something I just don't like to stay focused on it, I pass on it. And every time someone will say, oh my God I know exactly what you're talking about, I got it." So good ol' *Spirit* delivers messages for many people and Theresa doesn't have to talk personally to them. Maybe she's an all-purpose medium--what she says to others can and will apply to you!

Question 8 Who passed from a blood disease? She gets a response.

Question 9 Is it either from head to toe?

Question 10 Where does the liver come in?

Now there are big errors here.

A blood disease isn't located in one spot of the body. Blood circulates throughout the body so it naturally goes from head to toe. In addition, any blood disease always affects the liver.

Question 11 "Who's being tested for other things? Or for anything?"

IS THE LONG ISLAND MEDIUM THE REAL DEAL?

It seems like the "he" that she is talking to appears to be very confused and isn't giving her much to work with.

Questions 12 and 13 are a result of the confusion over the illness and testing. Okay, now it's time to see how many people are hit by the next question.

Question 14 "Who passed from a blow to the chest? It just labored my breathing. I couldn't breathe for like a second." No one is hit by it so Theresa quickly tosses out who died in front of someone.

She gets hits on questions 15, 16, and 17. She takes the safe route that the passed away dad is telling his daughter to release guilt over the passing. Who doesn't feel guilty about the passing of a parent, especially one that passes in front of you?

Question 18 references being "a sports fanatic." The daughter responds that he liked sports, another generic, safe question. Good play. However, Theresa doesn't let the daughter talk and brings in the fact that the deceased father admires the show's co-host, Michael Strahan. [Michael played for the New York Giants as a defensive end for fourteen years.] Then the daughter is brought back into the conversation as Theresa asks if she'd just celebrated a birthday or a special celebration. Why not pinpoint it down to just a birthday? If she's really talking with the departed father, he would certainly know his daughter's birthday. But that's not to be. Instead, the daughter says it wasn't her birthday but her mother-in-law recently had a birthday and she points to the woman sitting two seats over. Theresa is happy that the woman is wearing a Giants shirt as it helps validate her shtick. How unusual is it for someone to wear a Giants shirt on the show? Especially as it was filmed during football season in New York City?

Question 19 about a personal celebration is a safe question as we celebrate so many different days.

Question 20 is another medical question about someone who passed from an aneurism, brain tumor, or Alzheimer's.

Theresa says it has to be a female. Why? Because females are more likely to cry. She asks three questions: 21, 22, 23, and gets decent hits [but nothing odd]. The 24th is about the letter H—Helen, Hank, Harry? Nope. Theresa doesn't want to end on a bad note so she quickly moves on even though Kelly told her it was to be the last reading.

Question 25 "Who just died?" No response.

Question 26 "I feel like someone just died two weeks ago." Nope.

Question 27 "Two months ago?" That gets a response from a man but listen to the next thing she says.

Question 28 "I feel like unexpected but you were prepared but you weren't prepared." Which one is it, Theresa?

Question 29 "Are you the only son or the oldest son?" Hedge those bets!

She claims he had a loving relationship with his mother. Theresa is building the person up.

Notice at the 7:59 mark the "BYE" sign held up by the co-host.

She asks at least 30 questions in 8 minutes and 54 seconds, which averages out to about 2.8 per minute.

CHAPTER 7
PAST LIFE REGRESSION – REAL OR NOT?

This year the producers have decided that Theresa Caputo can't just be a medium. Of course, Theresa has to be an exceptional psychic/medium/chaneller selected by "somebody" to carry out a mission of exposing the world to *Spirit* and talking to the dead like none other. Naturally, the Hicksville native doesn't talk to *Spirit* unless she's paid about $800 per hour. Thus, it's not only a special gift -- she must be special to have the gift.

Theresa Caputo and staff should spend more time reading the Bible. No place does it teach that having a gift from God is because you're a special being. Being granted a gift from God doesn't make you special due to having the gift. In reality, the opposite is true. If you think you're special, God is unlikely to give the gift to you. So who makes people feel like they have special gifts? That fallen angel who lurks in the shadow sure does.

She gives a false reading at a gas station. We debunked that one earlier on but let's look at the staging.

- When she arrives, Freddie is standing there texting, not actually pumping gas
- When she goes into the store to pay he's pumping gas
- When she comes out the guy is pumping gas
- When she starts to pump her gas he's pumping gas
- While she stands there doing her tongue in cheek thing he's pumping gas
- When she goes over to talk and give her reading he's still pumping gas

Theresa should've advised him to check his gas tank for a leak. Also, she had walked past this waiting man twice. Are spirits that polite as to wait until she's pumping gas to say that now is the time to communicate with the man?

She then meets Pat Longo for a meal at the Fuel Your Body Café.
http://www.fuelyourbodycafe.com/Main.html

Pat has been discussed earlier. Theresa admits that Pat is her spiritual healer or teacher or both and has been a friend for some time. She dances around the fact that Pat was the one who helped Theresa bring out her gift. Theresa just has to know *why me*? Why is this so important? According to Theresa, her gift is changing. She no longer sees things in symbols, as she demonstrated on the *Live with Kelly and Michael Show* back in September 2012. According to her, *Spirit* is actually entering her to communicate. Does that mean channeling is coming next season? Or is something more sinister taking place? Pat says that she will do a past life regression on her. Theresa informs the viewers that she feels that we've all lived many past lives.

Theresa claims she is Catholic. But she doesn't tell us how she can balance this with her faith. Nor does she try to explain how this works with the death of Christ. Christ paid the price for our sins and the many life thing.

Back in her home, Theresa's making a list of questions for this upcoming past life stuff. Larry acts as if she's never done it before.

But when Larry Jr. comes in the talk changes as she has done it in the past and is nothing surprising.

She goes to Pat Longo's home and we see that Pat uses guided mediation. Or you might call it self-hypnosis. What it really looks like is Theresa sitting on a recliner with her eyes closed and talking softly. Apparently, out of the numerous previous lives Theresa must have lived, she had three bad ones. In these bad past lives, she was blamed for things she didn't do. In one, she had her throat sliced open and then they hung her. In another, she was a very rich and powerful man. And if she was truly experiencing such horrific past lives, why doesn't her voice change? Why don't we get a deeper voice? An accent? A voice filled with fear?

Wouldn't it be helpful if she said her name was John Jones and she lived in Cardiff, Wales from 1549 to 1602? That would be impressive. Alternatively, if she lived as a man in Lyon, France in the 18th century, that might make it more convincing. But we get no dates, no names, no country or countries. Nothing is revealed that would allow us to check and validate her claims. Theresa wants us to buy it so we think she has suffered so much that now she has the power to heal people. Pat Longo already claims she heals people even through the power of A T & T and other phone service providers.

But they can't let a simple past life regression be the only thing. They need to bring in Pat's dead husband, Vinnie, who died recently of cancer. Again, why wasn't Pat able to heal him?

At the end of the session, Theresa claims she has completely changed. Cue waterworks to help sell it.

Also, Theresa says that many people in her family have the gift. Why wasn't this ever mentioned before? Why not talk to those family members about the gift? Will we be seeing her children channel on upcoming seasons of *The Long Island Mediums*? What if Larry suddenly learns how to channel after having a NDE? Or maybe there aren't any real gifts within the family except to make money deluding the gullible?

Here is a great post on the subject of past life regression and how it's not real:

http://www.skepdic.com/pastlife.html

CHAPTER 8
THERESA TAKES ON THE SUNSHINE STATE

Traveling through Florida, Theresa blazed a trail just north of Miami and what we uncovered was ... well, read on!

If you've tried to book an appointment with Theresa, you know there's a wait of up to three years. Many fans would love for other fans to cancel so they can skip ahead in that line and have a reading with Theresa. She receives thousands of emails filled with sob stories concerning the demise of loved ones, and how the one left behind is in pain. Having a huge surplus of people wanting readings, but not able to get one creates a backlog. Nor does it increase that bank account. It's also detrimental for the production company as fans get restless and stop watching the show. Or they might find another, less expensive but less known medium.

So, why not send Theresa to a scenic location to meet some of her adoring fans? She gets a free trip out of the deal, as do some of the more desperate fans with riveting stories. The production company makes it more fun for the viewers as they stage, and we really mean stage, quite a road show.

They gave the viewer so many details that it was very easy to visit all the locations and learn from staff and management just what this was all about. You know what makes Theresa and company tick? Ratings, money, and fame, baby!

First location
Pelican Grand Resort in Fort Lauderdale

http://www.pelicanbeach.com/

For a resort with a great ocean view, it's reasonably priced and the food isn't bad, either. However, what we learned from talking to staff and management is far different from what the viewer saw on TV.

According to what was seen on TV:

Theresa Caputo left behind her family and her comfort zone of Long Island to travel to Southern Florida. This selfless medium flew 1,300 miles to do readings for her fans. Once there, Theresa drives a white rental SUV to the Pelican Grand Resort. Melanie is on a girl's weekend with her sister-in-law, Melissa, and three other women. Pregnant Melanie recently lost her husband and desperately needs to hear from him. Melissa contacted Theresa to see if that was possible. To lighten up the episode, Theresa delivers room service and surprises Melanie in her room. Melanie gets a reading. Everything is great and wonderful and Melanie is touched to learn about her husband's passing and afterlife.

What really took place?

We talked to the employees who work behind the front desk, in the kitchen, and the cleaning staff. Here's what really took place.

• Production company employees had been in contact with the resort for some time. They visited the resort, and looked over the rooms and other interiors they would shoot in. Outside of the resort was scouted for the place to do the interviews and much of the exterior scenes were shot prior to Theresa's arrival.

• When arriving at the resort, Theresa was told to go to the kitchen where room service was prepped. The staff was ready for her, as they knew she would be filming there.

• The women in the room were notified that she was coming up with the breakfast.

• Melanie knew she had to be the one to open the door, say, "Shut up!" and close it. Of course, she had to pretend to be flummoxed. She also spoke with the other guests about what was going to take place, as they all had to sign agreements in order to be seen on the show.

• The taping of the reading and remarks from Melinda and Melissa took most of the day to film. It was shot in different areas of the suite. Breaks were taken to make sure that all involved were getting the biggest bang for the buck.

• The production team was overheard laughing at how the viewers would be fooled by this one.

Second location
Theresa and Larry visit Yo Mamas Ice Cream

http://www.popscorn.com/icecream.html

According to what was seen on TV:

Theresa and Larry, happy looking tourists, swing by for some ice cream. They are amazed at the selection of ice cream treats. Theresa just can't make up her mind about what to order. But wait, something tells her to do a reading for the teenager behind the counter. The gal misses her grandmother and the death made such an impact, the employee runs out of the store – but soon returns. After Theresa tells the gal how much granny loved her, all is well and the happy New Yorkers depart, with Larry holding a tin of popcorn.

What really took place?

Nobody Screamed for Ice Cream at Yo Mama's Ice Cream!

This reminds us of our work breaking down fake scenes in such shows as *Paranormal State*, *Psychic Kids: Children of the Paranormal*, and the *Haunted Collector*. This is due to the fact that what the viewers think took place really didn't.

Shots throughout the scene don't match.

We visited the shop and talked to Lonnie and Lee Feldman, the brothers who own the shop, their employees, and those working in neighboring stores.

Production company workers contacted the shop days before the shooting took place. One of the stipulations was that a staff member needed to have a compelling story. A loving grandmother who couldn't enjoy food due to her poor health was deemed to be appropriately moving.

Larry and Theresa never bought any ice cream. This appears to be true from breaking down the scene. Of course, Theresa acted like she's an ice cream fanatic on camera, helping sell her story, and makes her look like a confirmed sweets lover. This is done because her fan base can relate to loving ice cream. Theresa is only seen standing in one area—near the cash register. An ice cream fan would walk up and down the length of the nicely displayed frozen treats, noting the array of flavors. The ice cream isn't cheap, they sell it by the pound and encourage you to get lots of heavy toppings like cookies, granola, nuts, and candy.

Watch the background as the number of people in the store changes from three, to two, to one and back to two. You'll also see some shots of the owners in the background.

During the reading, the counter girl said she never talked about her grandmother's death to anyone. Also, her grandmother died when she was seven-years-old.

Theresa loudly asks owner about who had someone who died of throat cancer? We see a shot of the counter girl and the manager says "Yeah." [Odd, the young lady never told anyone, but the owner also gives her a glance as if to say that's your cue].

This is why she and her husband never looked at the ice cream selections near the area where the girl was standing--they didn't want her on camera yet.

We're now shown the girl and Theresa embarks on the staged reading.

Note: We have to wonder the logic of the statement she makes to the girl: "I'm not asking you to believe in what I do as it doesn't matter if you do." Really? Does that mean that if I don't believe what you're telling me, I can't accept anything that you say.

The girl becomes upset and leaves, running across the street. She later returns.

The shot of her talking about how she now believes Theresa but still doubts others and her feelings over the death of her grandmother was filmed later that day.

Third location
15th Street Fisheries & Dockside Cafe

http://www.15streetfisheries.com/

Located inside the Lauderdale Marina, this restaurant has great views and is a fish and boat lover's paradise. When we arrived, we went right to the bar as drink loosens lips of serving staff, management, and customers. The food here is very good but pricey.

According to what was seen on TV:

Young widow Heidi and son Jacob are grieving over the death of his father. A surprise reading from Theresa, courtesy of Heidi's sister, Katie, is just the remedy.

Theresa knows two diehard fans by their delighted reactions. "I came from Long Island just to surprise you!" says Theresa. They go to an empty upstairs dining room for a reading in which she tells them how much he misses them, how much he did for the son, and how much he loved Heidi.

What really took place?

Everything was staged at the restaurant. Theresa drives up and gets Doris Day parking. The production company worked closely with the restaurant management to seat the trio in the back part of the restaurant so she could strut through the place, in effect doing a tour.

The scene where she tells the customers to be quiet with a loud "shhhhh" wasn't even close to where they sat.

Notice the two sisters and boy dining at the table. Yet why are there four beverage glasses on the table? The boy has a fresh drink with a straw that still has a bit of the wrapper on the top.

The table where the threesome is dining has a window behind it. In one shot, you'll notice there is no one at the window. However, as soon as Theresa arrives, you'll see someone wearing a long sleeved black shirt and the telltale sign of a boom operator [someone holding a microphone on a short pole].

During the interaction between Theresa and the three seated at the table, the boy's glass level changes and can be seen as half empty and almost empty.

The fourth glass disappears just before the end of the scene.

They go upstairs to a private dining area. The reading and the reaction shots take up most of the day, not the hour that she told Katie. Then again, how much time does Theresa spend with the clients before the reading? If you go by this video of Howard Stern, we learn that it's 45 minutes of alone time [where priming is done] with no cameras between Theresa and the client[s].
http://scifake.com/howard-stern-dislikes-mediums-including-long-island-medium/

The staff who worked that day report that Theresa was reminded of what things to point out during the reading by the production crew.

Also, she shows off some classic cold reading lines. These are usually affirmations.

- They wish you a happy birthday is always a standard line.
- Their soul will be with you is another.
- Theresa tells the boy that his father will be there when he gets his baseball uniform. Notice how she adds to it to make it fit the reading.
- I am sorry [says the dearly departed].
- I didn't suffer and I passed away quickly. Again, a common affirmation.
- Please don't be angry with me is another one.
- You were my soul mate and I appreciate everything you ever did for me.

Whenever you hear a medium say such affirmations you know you're getting a cold reading.

As long as Theresa says great things about the

deceased man, his name isn't revealed, that's all that matters. Jacob is an adolescent. Before boys turn into teenagers, they usually have fond memories of their fathers. Also, the boy has a camera pointed at him, a doting mother who he has to live with after this episode airs, and a live wire medium hovering across the table from him. What's a kid to do? Agree that dad was all that and more.

Two things to note: and we really wonder why they allowed this to slip through editing.

1. Heidi said her husband had internal bleeding and that his stomach filled with blood. He was taken to the hospital and later died. Theresa says that he died "instantly." That directly contradicts what Heidi said.

2. Heidi says her dead husband loved his kids [plural] yet the only message he sent was to her son. We see a photograph of the family and there are two boys shown. Did Theresa not know about his older son?

Heidi's father had passed away yet apparently he didn't send any messages or none were shown.

Theresa asks the boy if he felt angry when his father passed away. There is nothing unusual about that.

Fourth location
M. Cruz Rentals at Hugh Taylor Birch State Park

http://www.mcruzrentals.com

The Hugh Taylor Birch State Park is a located in the middle of Fort Lauderdale and is well worth visiting. Right at the park's entrance, you'll see the M. Cruz

Rentals, owned by Brent Wysocki.

According to what was seen on TV:

Theresa and Larry took a Segway tour through the park and at one point pause to admire an enormous Banyan tree. [This is the type of tree Buddha sat under to gain enlightenment.] Theresa gives Brent a reading.

What really took place?

We talked to his staff and once again, the production company contacted M. Cruz Rentals long before Theresa and Larry arrived. They set everything up. It seems that Brent was going through a tough time in his life. So the production company shared the details, thinking this would cheer him up and help the rental business that had been off lately. The crew set up at the Banyan tree as they felt it would make a great background for the reading.

Fifth location
The Twin Salon in North Miami Beach

http://thetwinsalon.com/

According to what was seen on TV:

Wendy is concerned about her cousin Sandi's well-being and contacted Theresa with the hope of getting her a reading. Sandi has sadly endured her only daughter's murder. Will a reading change her life and as Theresa says, "Give her life back and give her hope."

What really took place?

- It seems that Theresa got lost and couldn't find the entrance to the back parking lot. Hey, where's *Spirit* when you need him? So she meets Wendy late but not as late as they pretend.

- Everyone knew what's about to happen. Some say even Sandi knew, as there is one shot of her looking out the window as Theresa pulls up in front of the salon.

- They actually ran paying customers out of the shop. Theresa says, "Wrap it up here so we can get this reading underway."

A lot of information is revealed before the reading as Wendy says:

- Sandi has recently suffered a devastating loss
- Sandi has been devastated
- Sandi has been through a tough time during the last two years
- She is staying with me for the next two months
- She hasn't worked in two years
- She cries every day
- She barely eats, barely sleeps

The reading is lame. No details given in the reading about the murder, and it was all very general. What parent wouldn't want to hear that their child was at peace?

Theresa is not at the top of her game in this one. Sandi reveals that it's been two years, two days, and two hours since the murder. This woman needs professional mental health therapy. If Sandi chooses to go with new age thinking, she'd be taught that her behavior actually prevents her daughter from finding peace on the other side.

Theresa offered nothing other than platitudes.

People there said Theresa was in a hurry to get the reading finished.

Sixth location
Tennis anyone?

http://cliffdrysdale.com/locations/weston-tennis-center

With a few moments left in the show, the Caputos' are off to play some tennis. They just have to share Theresa's gift with their coach, Steven, and he learns how his dear friend feels his pain. They then go off, as Larry wants a cool drink and later Theresa and husband walk down a path.

What really happened? Yes, they played tennis. Yes, Larry had a few cold ones, and yes, they took a walk. What they didn't tell you was that the production team asked around about who was going to be Theresa's coach. Guess *Spirit* was at the beach sipping margaritas that day.

CHAPTER 9
MISINFORMATION IN THE LAND OF [DR.] OZ

Theresa Caputo joins to the land of Dr. Oz and brings a lot of bad science with her.

Dr. Mehmet Oz is one of those authorities that hold sway over the public because Oprah Winfrey used to have him on her show. He has a medical degree from the University of Pennsylvania School of Medicine [1986] and a Masters degree from the Wharton School. He has written several bestselling health-related books. However, what sets him apart is that he has fully embraced lots of new age wackiness. His wife is a "Reiki Master," which is yet another bogus new age healing method. Read more about Reiki by another doctor, Stephen Barrett, M.D.
http://www.quackwatch.com/01QuackeryRelatedTopics/reiki.html

Due to the popularity of her TLC show, Theresa Caputo is now welcome on other shows. Therefore, when she wants on a big show, she's able to get on a big show and promote her shtick and try to overwhelm skeptics with her amazing talents. She wants the world to see what goes on inside her head though nothing's mentioned about whether her brain flashes money signs.

Dr. Oz tells the medium that she is a brave woman. Pretending to be puzzled, she asks why? He tells her they'll hook her brain up to display what takes place during her readings. Maybe there will be a lot of activity, maybe not.

Theresa says it doesn't matter because her gift helps people. That's why she's there – to help people, she claims. By the way it really wasn't her idea but *Spirit's* idea to do this [*Spirit* must be the best agent in the world]. Of course, and he wouldn't do this unless it helps add money to that growing bank account.

They ask her to do a reading and she claims her heart is pounding. Why doesn't Dr. Oz verify this?

She gets very specific on what she's picking up:

~ A father has stepped forward

~ A daughter is there to talk

~ Something to do to the chest or a blow to the chest [we heard all of this in the reading from *Live With Kelly and Michael*]

There is confusion in the audience concerning whom this message is directed to.

And Theresa seems to be confused. No longer is she saying daughter, as she now says a father and a young girl.

But more confusion begins to set in as a woman claiming the father sits down for her on-stage reading.

Now Theresa tries selling more of her skills by claiming that she can read other people's emotions. Only sociopaths can't do this.

She goes on a tear about someone passing and uses the phrase "at that exact moment." No one ever expects a person to die at an exact time, like 12:06 p.m., unless they're being executed. People pass at times that we can't ever know.

She then goes on her "piggybacking" thing as she claims she has no power to control who steps forward, what they say, and more importantly, what they don't say. This is her handy escape clause. There's confusion because more than one person lost their dad. This confusion could be avoided by asking the spirit his name! More than one person states that they have lost a daughter. By using her name, the correct mother could identify her daughter.

This alleged message really casts doubts on her claims. She asks [observe that very little telling is going on here] the woman about the daughter. But the woman uses the term HE and not she. Theresa asks the woman if they played a role in making decisions on the passing of the dad and she says yes. Most people would say yes.

At the end of the reading, it's clear that she spent all her time with only one of the women, and the other one simply sat there.

Dr. Daniel Amen is introduced and Dr. Oz claims

IS THE LONG ISLAND MEDIUM THE REAL DEAL?

that they are about to prove that Theresa and others who make the same claims are really talking to dead people. That isn't what's being proven. The only thing being done is that a brain image is going to be taken--is it a scan or a scam? According to this article, Harriet Hall M.D. examines SPECT scans: http://www.quackwatch.org/06ResearchProjects/amen.html

Here's another article about how these scans are actually a costly pseudo-science: http://www.sciencebasedmedicine.org/spect-scans-at-the-amen-clinic-a-new-phrenology/

They also confuse the terms medium and channeling. The medium relays messages from the dead to the living. The channeler claims they allow a spirit or spirits to enter them and speak to the living. Therefore, a medium and a channeler are two very different things.

Most people don't know about brain imaging and the areas of the brain that light up. This show feeds off the audience's ignorance and helps in the deception that Dr. Oz and the Long Island Medium are doing.

They come up with some test in which if you respond to with positives means you're more likely to be psychic. Who established the criteria for this test? We aren't told. What was the scientific process that established that this test is legitimate? Again, nothing. But here we go with the test, and out of the three questions, all of them are what they are looking for.

1. History of anxiety - what level are you looking for? A little, a lot? How often? She indicates she's anxious.

2. Unusual spiritual or religious experiences? What

is an unusual religious experience? Well, whatever it must be, Theresa stakes her claim that she has them.

~ She has seen things [no examples given].

~ She has heard things [no examples given].

~ Seen the Virgin Mary [Is that odd? How many non-Catholics and Catholics have seen her?].

~ The presence of God in some of her readings. [God is always there, she's just trying to sound special].

3. Family history of psychic phenomena? This question is so bad we could write a book on it. How do you prove any of the past claims to be real?

4. History of brain trauma? What type and to what region of the brain?

In a few seconds, Dr. Amen is going to tell us all about the different parts of the brain and what they do. This information is learned over the course of a few years in college, but hey, Dr. Oz only has incredible people on his show...

Dr. Amen talks about two sections of the brain:

- Temporal lobe
- Prefrontal cortex

He claims the stimulus of the temporal lobe causes people to FEEL a presence. Not to see a presence but to feel a presence. There's no description of what type of presence, just a sensation of a presence.

http://en.wikipedia.org/wiki/Temporal_lobe

This area is part of the auditory system that gives us the ability to understand and process language into memory. If this area's stimulated, feeling a presence is only logical as you're preparing to hear language and create a memory. It has absolutely nothing to do with spirits.

http://en.wikipedia.org/wiki/Prefrontal_cortex

The cortex is responsible for behavior. Understanding the results of that behavior has nothing to do with seeing or hearing anything.

We're told she gave a young woman a reading. What were the results?

The temporal lobe is stimulated which is normal as Theresa asks questions. Information is fed back to it so she can pull memories. Was this information she had learned earlier about this girl and is recalling it?

Reduction in activity in the frontal lobe is where your rational and moral thinking takes place. Reduction would mean the brain [person] is comfortable with what is being done, therefore it's satisfying to Theresa--not frightening whatsoever.

They fail to address the high levels of anxiety in her life. That would really affect anyone trying to meditate, especially someone who states, "I'm living proof of anxiety."

After a 15-minute session, the doctors are able to prove that Theresa is some kind of prophet! In chapter 2 we showed what she would have to do to be one and she clearly misses the mark in the prophet category.

To say this proves anything would make you the laughing stock of the scientific community. Hundreds, if not thousands, of such tests would need to be done along with testing males and females from around the world under the same conditions.

Dr. Oz jumped the shark years ago, now he has jumped into the lake called No Credibility.

CHAPTER 10
PLANTS IN THE SPOTLIGHT

When doing an investigation like this you have to devour anything written or posted to gather as much information as you can to get the full story. Blogs, videos, interviews, forums, all of it sheds light on the subject you're researching.

I recall when we were uncovering the story about fake paranormal reality shows like *Paranormal State, Psychic Kids: Children of the Paranormal, The Haunted Collector*, and others, that we watched some episodes 50, 60, even 100 times. Each time we picked up something new.

One day I was watching a video clip of Theresa on *The Ellen Show*. It's very short and concerns the reading of a woman by Theresa. Larry and Larry Jr. were sitting in the audience. It goes by very quick so if blink, you'll miss the fact that she [the person being read] is nothing more than a plant.

The clip in question was posted by Ron Tebo, the

man behind the website Scifake.com. For the past several years, he's exposed some of the same questionable people that we've gone after. Ron did a very good job of catching the plant in the audience. Also, this isn't the first time you've seen her in an audience where Theresa was giving readings.

http://scifake.com/video-proof-long-island-medium-is-a-fraud/#comment-23231

When she starts talking about someone who lost a child notice her hand gesture. Theresa extends her right palm out flat and circles the base of it with her left index finger.

Keep a close eye on her husband and son, Larry and Larry Jr. They aren't backstage, off to the side of the stage, or in the front row. Note that they're sitting in the same row that Theresa claims the message is for. Other audience members have raised their hands accepting the message even prior to Theresa acknowledging this woman. Both Larry's are looking to their left down the row at the woman wearing a blue shirt.

Just like Ron, I felt I'd seen her in another audience getting a reading from Theresa.

After looking through several videos, we found her. The plant appears to have made some minor cosmetic changes but if you watch both videos, you'll see this is the same woman.

http://www.youtube.com/watch?v=OzxCkGxipyI
Red-haired woman with brown glasses and crocheted white top seen from 2:19 to 2:54

http://www.youtube.com/watch?v=30B6NarCA98

Red-haired woman with similar brown glasses and a blue top seen from 0:18 to 0:43

We'd like to point out that at least six or seven months have passed since the *Live With Kelly and Michael* Show and *The Ellen Show*. This explains the slight changes in appearance.

NOTE: If the video links are no longer active, please contact freeallspirits@live.com and we'll send you a screenshot.

While we're on the topic of plants, what about planted information? Have you ever seen Theresa's ears during any of her events or group readings? In an individual reading, the information is easily remembered. However, during an event or on-camera group reading, it's much more difficult to keep seat locations and other bits of information in order.

If you attend her events, you aren't allowed to take photos or recordings allowed. What is she hiding? You're about to find out.

CHAPTER 11
LIVE WITH THERSA CAPUTO IN CERRITOS, CA

When starting an investigation into something that is suspicious, odd things start to happen. Books I need to read literally fall into my lap. People who have information I need come forward, and odd events take place. One of the oddest events was the time I spent in working class Cerritos to watch a blonde New Yorker weave a spell over a crowd of predominantly middle aged women.

I get a text message from a friend asking me if I'd heard of a medium named Theresa Caputo. I picked up the phone and was lucky to catch my friend.

Yes, I have doubts about her authenticity.

Did I want to see her in person?

I sure did.

He'd brought a pair of tickets for her upcoming

show in Cerritos and his friend couldn't go. Would I like to go?

You bet.

The day of the reading, we fought LA traffic to reach Cerritos a bit early so we could watch and learn from the crowd.

I was reminded of the scene from the 1960 science fiction film based on the H. G. Wells book, *The Time Machine.* If you aren't familiar with the movie [or story] in the future the few remaining people living above ground are called to come together by a blaring horn which turns them into robot like creatures.

The people approaching the center reminded me of those hapless people that I'd seen in that movie. They seemingly had unblinking eyes. The crowd consisted of mostly middle aged women to those in their senior years. They appeared to approach the auditorium with the reverence reserved for a visiting Pope.

"I'm going to free them."

"She'd better read me."

"I know my husband is here—I can feel him,"

"I've got to know my son is okay."

Some women were clutching photos; others had rosaries, and other mementoes of their loved ones.

"Not everyone was going to get a reading," my friend said.

Most of them are so deluded that they will. I told

him about Theresa's piggyback theory.

"It's not logical," he said.

True that and it's not real. Every relationship is different and no two people are exactly alike. As we get closer, the area near the entrance is increasingly crowded. The doors still haven't opened. Small groups begin to form as stranger meets stranger. They become an impromptu family bound by great sadness and a desire to hear from dead family and friends they have lost. I overhear snippets of conversation.

"Theresa Caputo is so real."

"I just love her so much."

"I would give up anything in my life just to get to a reading from her."

"She is so god-like."

"She's an angel sent from heaven."

My friend is appalled and says the same thing I'm thinking.

"What if a Christian prophet charged what she charges?" he asked, knowing the answer.

"He'd be run out of L.A. County."

I also started to notice some men and women who were nicely dressed and overly friendly as they moved around the clusters of Theresa Caputo fans. I noticed these individuals seemed to hone in on the more distraught appearing attendees.

I edge closer to one such group that is talking to one of these caring angels. I spot a man young enough to pass as a son or grandson of many of the attendees.

How did your brother die?

What were you doing when it happened?

Did you get to see him before he passed? Did you talk to him?

What happened to you after his death?

The concerned angel wanted to know where the woman was sitting. He asked if he could stop by and talk some more? The distraught woman tells him what area she and her friends are in and he nods and pulls away from the group.

Is this a plant? The person walks casually away mixing with the ever-growing crowd. We follow at a safe distance, as whoever this person is, they are good, occasionally glancing behind them.

We have almost circled the building 180 degrees. The concerned angel approaches a security line near the rear of the center, flashes something, and continues. We stop, knowing that we can't cross that line. So we turn around and head back to the front. By the time we reach the main entrance, the doors are now open and the crowd pours in.

No photos or recording devices are allowed.

No photos I can understand. I wouldn't want to try to talk with cameras going off for two straight hours. I recall seeing Ray Charles live and even though he was blind, you couldn't take any photos.

IS THE LONG ISLAND MEDIUM THE REAL DEAL?

But why no recording devices? That one was troubling. Well, here are four reasons:

1. To force people to rely on memory which is often unreliable.

2. If you listen to it again, you might not be as impressed as you were the first time.

3. If you match it up with other shows recorded in different cities it might sound alike.

4. Is it possible that they're afraid that you might pick up other voices? Like human voices [not spirit] speaking to her?

We notice as the center begins to fill that the omnipresent security, both uniformed and plainclothes, are keeping a close eye out on people they must fear have some sort of recording device.

Soon, we watch as Theresa Caputo minces onstage in those towering heels. She appears to be in less than a good mood as her comments are abrupt. The Long Island Medium claims that *Spirit* has many things to say and she goes right into it.

She goes to one area and asks who here lost a child? Yet she gets no reaction. She repeats herself twice, not getting a response.

Throughout the large auditorium, others wave their hands and some are about to jump out of their seats. However, she's not paying any attention to them. Why not?

1. Was someone who had a very compelling story

supposed to be in that area? Was she going to use this as a selling point for the show?

2. Was she given bad information?

This really upsets her. Apparently, some plans have been altered. What to do? Take it out on the ticket buyers. She seeks our admiration for her hair, her shoes, her dress and just being in the same room with her. She speaks of spirits, the church, and angels. Yet never once does she say anything about Jesus or the Holy Spirit.

There is a barrage of standard questions:

Who lost a husband?

Who lost a parent?

Who lost a loved one?

The rest of the night consists of nothing more than mostly good guesses and cold readings. Not once does she meet my gaze, in fact, she avoids men as much as she can--even if one raises his hand. In front of an older man with an upraised hand, Theresa ignores him and hones in on a fat middle-aged woman to read. Finally, the show ends and the crowd reacts to this woman with the big hair and overblown New York accent as if she cured cancer, AIDS, and worldwide famine. There is nothing humble about this woman.

The people departing are glassy eyed, empty of tears and full of hope and a new faith [fake hope and faith]. We walk out and notice a steady stream of people on their way to the back of the building.

Many approach her tour bus as if it's a UFO that

has flown her down to earth to give the world a new message. The beefed up security team makes sure that no one comes too close as touching the bus might kill you.

"Theresa! Theresa! Theresa!"

"We love you!"

"God bless you!"

Many cried out to her. Does she hear them? Does she care? Apparently not, as she never emerges from her luxury tour bus. After awhile the crowd departs. It's back to real life for them. But there are a few desperate women, some with flowers and gifts, who refuse to give up hope. I walk past a heavyset woman on the far side of fifty who is weeping uncontrollably.

"What will happen if I never see her again?"

"Nothing. You'd be better off." I say. She doesn't react. Was she in a false heaven worshiping Theresa Caputo who sits on a golden throne?

That thought is frightening and sends a chill down my back.

CHAPTER 12
WHO IS *SPIRIT*?

Just who or what the heck is Spirit? Don't ask Theresa – she doesn't know!

Spirit is just as important to the *Long Island Medium* show as Theresa Caputo is. Let's face it, if there was no *Spirit*, she wouldn't have an act. In order to answer the question about the mysterious *Spirit*, we have to approach it from two different sides of the issue.

1. Is *Spirit* fake?

2. Is *Spirit* real? If so, just who or what is it?

So let's address these two questions.

1. Is Spirit fake?

Let's discuss what I call Spiritual Socialism. This term means that every human being on the planet is on the same spiritual level as everyone else. No one is born with a special gift that makes him or her more spiritual than anyone else.

God doesn't create hyper-spiritual people. God can give spiritual gifts to people. Those that claim they've been given these gifts must put those gifts to the test. This isn't a test issued by an academic or a panel of skeptics. The test is made by God's rules and it is actually quite simple to determine.

A Does it fall in line with God's Word. If it doesn't then it's not real.

B Does it give all the glory to God and His Son the Lord Jesus Christ? If it doesn't, then it's not real.

So let's put *Spirit* to the test. Being a medium and talking to dead people are two things that God hates so it clearly doesn't fall in line with God's Word. Also, in any appearances seen on TV or a live show, have you seen Theresa or *Spirit* ever give the glory to God, mention the Lord Jesus Christ, or mention or quote Scripture? You haven't seen this.

Does it mean it's demonic? No. But it may very well be the figment of someone's wild imagination.

I often say that many start-up psychics, mediums, etc. often make huge claims about abilities they don't have, and they know they don't have ... yet. They keep telling the lie repeatedly, so they begin to believe the fake story is real.

Throughout our research, we've heard this term *Spirit* turned into the spirit, and spirits. That implies that a spirit or spirits are feeding her the information. So are there many spirits allegedly speaking to her? Are they always there?

It seems *Spirit* has a way of changing as the mood hits Theresa--or whether the cameras are rolling.

We see this very often in new age books, which are published as nonfiction. For example, Sylvia Browne can have conversations with dead celebrities as she reveals in her book, *Past Lives of the Rich and Famous*. How do you validate the "fact" that Bob Hope allegedly lived 56 lives? You can't! So new age authors can mingle fact with fiction and there will always be suckers, um, readers, who buy every word they write. The authors know that. The publishers know that. Unfortunately, the reader oftentimes doesn't know that they're being fed lies or they're too deluded to care.

Here are a few new age authors and some interesting insight into their theories, their books, and their lives.

The Dark Legacy of Carlos Castaneda
http://www.salon.com/2007/04/12/castaneda/

Lynn V. Andrews is a female version of Mr. Castaneda. Ms. Andrews writes about the fictional Sisterhood of the Shields in a dozen books
http://www.skepdic.com/andrews.html

T. Lobsang Rampa – Makes a mockery of Tibetan Buddhism and exploits the walk-in theory to the max by claiming to be one.
http://www.museumofhoaxes.com/hoax/archive/permalink/the_third_eye_of_t._lobsang_rampa

A runaway myth of the *Law of Attraction* has spawned loads of books, including *The Secret* and accompanying sequels.

List of New Age "Law of Attraction" Teachers: http://www.newagedeception.com/new/free-resources/20-list-of-new-age-qlaw-of-attractionq-teachers.html

Note that convicted murderer Jodi Arias utilized *The Secret Diary: A Personal Workbook for Achieving Health, Wealth and Happiness*. This was before she viciously killed another follower of the book, Travis Alexander. Jodi stabbed him 29 times, sliced his throat, and shot him to make certain he was dead. How did that book help them?

Any author or new age teacher, more commonly both, can say so and so spirit brings the spirit of the dead to me and I share the information. How can such claims be proven? We can't travel to the spirit realm to confirm what's said. They know this and this allows them to boldly make their claims.

At times, Theresa refers to her spirit guides and angels as imparting the information. Does she know or have any idea of what's going on? No, as she claims she doesn't understand how the process works. So maybe there is some logic to that as if she gives an explanation then the doubters could take the claim to task. She also avoids making predictions.

The claims change all the time because Theresa "doesn't understand it." The same can be said of what this *Spirit* tells her the majority of the time it's all just feel good/the dead are at peace so the living should be too. "Your loved ones are safe and at peace." That is usually what she says. Such claims are difficult to disprove. If *Spirit* told her things about the present or the future then she could be pinned down and found lacking.

Which brings us to the second question.

Is *Spirit* real?

If so what can it be?

- An angel

Nope. We explained that *Spirit* can't be real [a kind spirit] as it doesn't glorify God since angels are sole creations of the Lord. What is feeding her thirst for communication is not an angel.

- A spirit guide

What are spirit guides? Even real spirit guides are entities that are dead and no longer of this world. By some means, they become so much smarter than other spirits of the dead.

However, watching most psychics/mediums at work, the spirit can't even come up with the most basic information of their previous lives.

Here's an example using a famous person to make it easier to illustrate as we can provide verifiable facts. Let's imagine it's 2010. Mrs. Dolores Hope, [who died in 2011] is the widow of actor/comedian Bob Hope. She consults a medium to find out how Bob's doing.

Though born in England he resided in the Toluca Lake area for more than six decades. He lived in a custom built home at 10346 Moorpark Street. The home had 8 bedrooms and 11 bathrooms.

Here are two links that give much more information about Bob.

http://en.wikipedia.org/wiki/Bob_Hope

http://www.bobhope.com/

So, Mrs. Hope wants to make sure it's Bob. She asks some basic questions that Bob should know instantly. Provided this is a medium that doesn't cheat by using the internet, public library or a fact checker, the medium should be able to have Bob answer the following questions.

1. Bob, where were you born?
Eltham, England. He could also state that it was May 29, 1903.

2. Where did we live?
Toluca Lake. 10346 Moorpark Street.

3. How many bathrooms did we have in our house?
Eleven.

4. What is your favorite sport?
Golf! That's why I wrote a book called *Confessions of a Hooker*.

5. How many children did we have and what are their names?
Four kids. Eleanora, Linda, William Kelly Francis, and Anthony.

Most widows won't be hearing their late husband mention a house with eleven bathrooms, but the above example clarifies the point that if you are truly having a conversation with someone who has passed over, they can effectively answer your questions and add additional information. Sure, a fake medium with no access to the correct spirit or to any spirit, could guess at the number of children, but generally, they don't because it's easy to miss.

However, with your average medium, when encountering wandering spirit guides, they are awash with just about any new age gobbledygook you'll ever encounter. Oftentimes they come from mystical places, ancient lands, or faraway planets in faraway galaxies. However, just like dead spirits they can't give you specifics on anything that you can verify. Spirit guides shouldn't communicate in symbols saying that a mouth of a deceased is encircled with chocolate and that's the symbol of a diabetic. No, it's the sign of someone with poor table manners. If that spirit guide is the real deal it should say in clear English [or Spanish or whatever the main language is] the facts in words, and not using silly pictograms.

Why is this? Are spirit guide[s] claims bogus? Can they just be creations of our minds to make us feel better about our spiritual state? If we are somehow important to the spiritual realm, so we are to the rest of the world.

They seem to be similar to reports of being a walk-in, something that never fades away. A walk-in is a so-called body whose soul has departed and a new one has entered often for reasons to carry out some kind of mission to change the world for the better. From a Christian point of view, walk-ins don't exist.

So if it's not an angel, not a spirit guide...then what can *Spirit* be?

A demon?

Maybe.

It's the most logical explanation and the reason is simple.

As Christians [being Catholic makes you a Christian], this means that Theresa Caputo is one. To be a Christian, one accepts the Lord Jesus Christ as your Savior and you look on Him as the only way through the pearly gates. For a Christian, there is no fear about what takes place on the other side. It's that simple.

When you die and you are saved, the last breath you take here in this life is followed by your first breath in heaven. It's not you that is there the you of the body and the you that was focused on things of this world. When you're in heaven, you are focused on things of the spirit. You're not a parent or child, son or daughter. You have none of these things over there. You'll know your relatives and friends, but they are not those things while in heaven.

And you can look from heaven to hell and see who is down there.

If you're not saved you go to hell – you've used your free will to do so.

And depending on your church, there might be a middle area called purgatory or limbo.

Theresa claims that she is Catholic who holds the majority of the Church's beliefs. Now she claims there is no hell. She claims that the spirit of a person is reborn repeatedly. True Catholics believe in heaven and hell. True Catholics don't believe in reincarnation.

What most mediums spout, and this includes Theresa, is actually confusion. We watch an anxiety-driven housewife from Hicksville pretend to channel loved ones. Or is she under demonic influence? Because demons exist to bring confusion to whatever they encounter. And if a confused person seeks assistance, they'll oftentimes visit mediums for clarity.

Demons love to mislead people. They'll delude them into feeling that no matter what they do and how they live, there will be no harmony on the other side when the light switch of life is flicked off. Cheat on your partner, steal, lie, take mind-altering drugs, etc., hey, it doesn't matter.

Have you ever heard a message from Theresa concerning sin in a person's life?

Have you ever heard from this *Spirit* that anyone has been reborn to a new life? Yet Theresa states this happens all the time.

What demons love to lie about is the message of the spirit that Theresa delivers. It also appears that she and *Spirit* aren't ever apart. She has stated in the past that it is always with her. This is akin to someone that has fallen under demonic influence. Unfortunately for us, Theresa seeks to bring others under the same influence.

Many of her followers so blindly watch her show and hang onto her words of faux solace. "Your loved ones are safe and at peace," says Theresa. And because she says it on a scripted reality TV show, because she says it on a talk show where she is guest-starring, and because she says it out loud in a middle-sized auditorium, well, it's just got to be true.

Found on one of Ms. Caputo's fan sites is this desperate plea for help:

"I hope you receive this. I am going crazy and am dying inside. My mother told me when she died to find a medium. I have watched your show and always watch it since I saw it the first time. I think my mother sent some of your messages to me. I have so many unanswered questions of my mother's death and dying. I am unable to move on. I am dealing with health problems and money problems and not having my mother help me through this is destroying me. I have three kids that need me but I can't go on. I need your help desperately so I can move on."

CHAPTER 13
DOES THERESA CAPUTO CAUSE HARM?

Our journey is almost over. We've taken you into the world of Theresa Caputo and have pulled down the walls in front of things that psychics, mediums and new agers prefer to have hidden. In the name of truth and honesty, they need to be revealed to the public.

It's no longer four in the morning. I'm no longer in that motel room where I spent the night in order to repair the damage of a false new age medium. The demonic thing isn't howling outside my door. Yes, it's out there somewhere waiting and lurking, seeking to do as much harm as it can. Like any demon, it seeks to destroy anyone that comes its way, allows it in and communicates with it. It's pleased that many people buy its lies.

It's name is *Spirit*. It is a seducing spirit. It comes to people directly and it can attach itself to a person that has the ability to reach tens, hundreds, thousands and more at a time. The message it spreads is that of seduction and destruction.

- Take that drink. Numb the pain. Don't worry about the cost it'll have on your life. Because your life is worthless.

- Drink that booze. It won't judge you, it'll never leave you, and it'll always be there to make you feel so good.

- Watch that porn movie. You don't need anyone else. With porn, you've got it all right in your mind.

- The dead are here to talk to you. Everything is fine on the other side. The dead are just waiting for you to come over.

- Hell? What's that? That's a myth made up to scare you. There is no hell.

- Don't worry, your life doesn't end when you die. You'll come back again and again and with fewer problems. That's right there is really no heaven either.

It can go on continuously. Demons like *Spirit* have an answer for every suffering, every ill, every heartbreak, and every pain. You don't have to follow God. You don't have to trust the Holy Ghost nor do you have to accept Christ and the Bible. After all, mere mortals wrote it so you don't really need to follow the rules.

That's the damage people like Theresa peddle. She, and those like her, steals much more than your money and time. They remove something that is firm and solid and ask you to try to stand with fluffy white clouds of nothingness beneath you.

What they teach is smoke and mirrors hype and false promises. They know when things fall apart you'll suffer the damage. Where will they be? Probably enjoying their newly renovated house. Or maybe in a new mansion sitting in front of a roaring fireplace sipping martinis. Their surroundings are plush and fancy, built and paid for and by you and your suffering. But that thought won't cross their minds.

One of Theresa's enthusiastic followers posted a blog that stated that if you don't buy what Theresa's selling you have no right to challenge her claims. You had no right to say anything about whether she has a gift or not. Another misguided blogger wrote that if what she says is real or fake it doesn't matter. If it makes you feel good there can be no harm done.

They are reciting the false idea of personal truth. That means because I think someone is real or good, it makes it so, because I think it is. Sadly, personal truth can easily equal personal deception. Deceiving yourself is the worst thing you can do to yourself because you're living a lie.

If you've ever been married or in a relationship, you've forged a bond of trust. You say, "My partner is faithful and true to me. They love me and wouldn't cheat on me." Years go by and the relationship isn't thoroughly questioned or tested. But eventually it comes to light that the partner, the one they trusted implicitly, lied and cheated throughout the duration of the relationship. Now the best years are behind them and they have nothing due to believing in a false personal truth.

If a false new age teacher says, "Friend there is no heaven and no hell," and you buy it making it your personal truth, who is to blame? When you die your spiritual eyes open expecting to find a paradise, but you find you've been lied to as you see nothing but hills and valleys filled with flames. What does your spirit do?

And, since you swallowed the teacher's lies with a hook, line and sinker mentality, you convinced others to buy into this personal truth ... you'll have others that will soon discover it's a lie.

Another reason why Theresa's program hurts the public is that its popularity means that many networks are looking for their own version of such a show.

This winter, Biography Channel ran a pilot of a show called *Supernatural Sisters*. It focused on two psychic sisters from Atlantic City, New Jersey, who do readings and ghost hunting investigations. Cathy Roller is the married sister who has a husband and a son and daughter that are close in age to Caputo's children. Cathy does group readings and spontaneous readings for people she meets on the street. She is a stay-at-home mom who does readings in her dining room. She's loud, brassy and has peroxide blonde hair sprayed into a poufy coiffure. Her resemblance to Theresa Caputo is uncanny. Her psychic-in-training sister, Laura Johnson, is a little quieter and more in the background. Luckily, we caught the program right after it aired and went to work, pointing out numerous errors that were seen in the hour-long show. For example, Cathy claims that dust only moves up and down. Here's our review of the show:
http://eyeontheparanormal.blogspot.com/2013/02/issue-104-supernatural-sisters-aka.html

The Biography Channel has banished intelligent programming in order to embrace para-reality TV shows and true crime programs. The Happy Medium, one of the psychic girls affiliated with Pat Longo, hosts *The Haunting Of*. Each week, a D-list celebrity claims they've been haunted. No problem! The Happy Medium quickly brings the haunting to an end.

As *Paranormal State* and *Ghost Hunter*s spawned copycats, so will *Long Island Medium*. Theresa will need to ramp it up more as they have to give them something fresh. This means that you can expect any semblance of truth to be sent packing.

This is the damage that Theresa Caputo and others like her do to you.

Maybe they have the best intentions. Maybe they really think what they're saying is true. However, that gives them no excuse to use the overused phrase the road to hell is paved with good intentions. In this case, it's way too accurate.

When a therapist sits down with a client, they have all sorts of ethical standards and government regulations to follow. If they violate these, they face legal actions. With a new age teacher, a psychic, a medium, a guru, or a spiritual counselor, there aren't any regulations. Outside of committing sexual assault or committing fraud, little can be done.

That psychic, medium, etc. can make up anything or repeat what they were taught to say and are free to do so. Because if they claim to be a spiritual counselor or doing readings is part of their religion, the First Amendment protects them.

Maybe so. And they might get away with it here. But what about on the other side? The side they claim to know about? Or are cagey enough to pretend not to know about? No matter, over there they won't find such foolishness. Because over there is a judge they can't escape.

What about the clients? There is no do over. There are no second chances. You can't mouth the defense "it sounded good." You can't claim that they seem so nice, so knowledgeable, so loving, so full of personality...

They may be good ringleaders and have bubbly personalities. And once they've finished taking your money they've moved on. It's you standing in front of the judge waiting to hear your sentence. No psychic or medium will go to the cross for you. Your time is up; the money has been collected. Now move on so the next victim can step in and take your place.

No teacher will offer himself or herself to be nailed on the cross for you. Hey, they write [or more likely have someone else write] their books, entertain you once a week courtesy of their TV show, make things up, or twist around some ancient lies they've been taught. You paid for the book, you invest your time in their show, and you bought a ticket for the class or seminar. You got what you paid for...what the hell do you expect other than "Your loved ones are safe and at peace." That's the problem, you don't know if your loved ones are or aren't safe and at peace, do you? However, you will realize that you aren't safe and you're not at peace.

No medium will shed their blood for you and even if they did it doesn't cover any sin they ever committed or any of your sins. Because a psychic, medium, whatever is no different from you.

No TV personality can speak for the Lord God. They

can say there's no heaven or hell, but that doesn't make it true. Who is more trustworthy--the personality or God? At least His program is never in rerun status, never canceled, and never off the air.

The damage caused by mediums isn't just affecting this generation. It affects future generations. Your children, grandchildren, great-grandchildren to come will hear the same false words and repeat the same false personal lies.

It's time to bring this foolishness to an end. Turn to someone that's there for you all the time. He is there with a truth that will always be true and He will always be there. The Word of God is free and best of all; it will always set you free.

CHAPTER 14
CONFUSION

The story of what's really going on with Theresa Caputo and her success seems to get deeper and deeper, and as it does the confusion keeps growing.

This a normal ploy when people or TV programs [fake or scripted reality shows] will toss out red herrings to keep folks like us who are seeking to expose the truth. It's done to keep the inquisitive off track and takes time away from following the true leads.

If *Spirit* stays with her 24/7 as she claims "*Spirit* is always with me" one of the demons that might be buddy-buddy with *Spirit* is called the Jezebel sprit. It's a master of creating confusion and decent people can't discern who is working this evil. The Jezebel spirit wears a mask and this allows it the ability to seduce and deceive people.

It all begins with the Caputo family. You have a loving Italian-American New York family that has many parallels to the fictional HBO series *The Sopranos*.

Theresa is Carmela

Larry is Tony

Larry Jr. is Tony Jr. [AJ]

Victoria is Meadow

The Caputos are seen as a loving and caring family. Mom is a Medium with big hair and a bigger personality, dad is devoted to her, and so are the young adult son and daughter. How could such nice people be up to no good? Many viewers of the fictional show *The Sopranos* didn't find Tony evil, no matter how many times he swindled and killed people; no matter how many extramarital affairs he had. Ultimately, he was viewed as a dad who was doing what he had to do to get by.

When we were wrapping up the investigation into the Long Island Medium, we stumbled across an odd website devoted to her. We haven't determined if it's a joke or not. If so, it's in very poor taste, as false claims are found and a real human being is used to sell the product. Or is money at the root of it?

Here is the page in question:

http://www.theresacaputofake.com/

We uploaded screen shots to it in case the website becomes disabled.

http://eyeontheparanormal.blogspot.com/p/fake-caputo-book.html

IS THE LONG ISLAND MEDIUM THE REAL DEAL?

The Theresa Caputo Diaries seems to be a book that brings into question claims concerning her abilities and whether she really is the real deal, according to the author Dr. James L. Pendergast.

The only issue is that there is nothing real in the claims made on this page! We fact checked every detail about this alleged book.

- There is no such expose coming out by that title. There is no listing outside of this one website, which is called theresacaputofake.com. Amazon and Barnes and Noble don't have *The Theresa Caputo Diaries* listed.

The pull quote from the New York Times: "A triumph. Dr. Pendergast is prolific and uncompromising." In July, it was changed to "The Times," a London newspaper.
http://www.thetimes.co.uk/tto/news/

Neither newspaper has the review quoted, never heard of the book or of a James L. Pendergast.

- There is a National Book Award. However, there isn't a National Book Review Award. In June, there was a gold seal for the Best Books Award Winner from USA Book News, but no such book is listed as the 2013 winners haven't been chosen yet.

- Notice three reviews of the book

"The Telegraph"

http://www.telegraph.co.uk/

We contacted them and they have never heard of the

book never reviewed the book and have never heard of or ever ran a story on a Dr. James L. Pendergast

"Psychology Today"

http://www.psychologytoday.com/

As of early July, the webmaster of the page has removed the Today from the title to create a nonexistent "Psychology" magazine. Needles to say, no one affiliated with "Psychology Today" ever heard of a Dr. James L. Pendergast. Suffice it to say, they never ran any story on him, his work, or ever featured a photo of him.

"The Christian Science Monitor"

http://www.csmonitor.com/

No one affiliated with "The Christian Science Monitor" has heard of the book and never reviewed it. They weren't familiar with the good doctor and never ran a story on him. The newspaper name was later changed to "The Christian Monitor."

Now we really get a merging of fact and fiction.

They tell [sell!] the story of Dr. James L. Pendergast by mentioning he's a leading expert in the fields of psychology and psychiatry. Touted as having 30 years worth of tenure at both Harvard and Cambridge Universities, this combination is an academic's wet dream. We see a photo of the doctor at one of his very well attended speaking engagements from 2011.

The problem here is that the picture you see isn't of the esteemed Dr. James L. Pendergast. Not at all. This photo shows Sir Ken Robinson [no relation!]. He is a professor of education who was born in Liverpool. If you'd like to learn more, here's his official website: http://sirkenrobinson.com/

Sir Ken Robinson is a "New York Times" bestselling author; he has a PhD, and is highly regarded in the field of education.

Pendergast, a supposed leader in the field in psychology and psychiatry doesn't exist, as we consulted numerous search engines based in America and the UK. There are no books, no research, no lectures, no articles, no TV appearances and no radio interviews for Pendergast.

Again, a 30-year tenure at both Harvard and Cambridge Universities is really in doubt and we were able to verify that no such individual has those credentials.

Writing 22 bestselling books is something Dr. Pendergast hasn't done.

According to the text, we learn that the good doctor has made "groundbreaking new discoveries in understanding of the human brain..." Well, the best we can ascertain is that maybe this Pendergast character has dug a hole or two, but no news story leads us back to his name. The American Psychiatric Association [APA] has no information on him and he hasn't spoken at or presented any research at any APA conference or convention.

A popular lecture tour that over 100,000 attendees have attended can't be proven as there is nothing anyplace about such a tour.

Claims of a "sensationally popular" TV show on the

Discovery UK channel? Wouldn't the show's name be mentioned? Wouldn't there be quotes about it from TV critics? Another fictitious claim.

The webpage states he was interviewed by the "Los Angeles Times"[http://www.latimes.com] on May 23, 2013 concerning the book. The issue we have shows no such story on that day or any other. No information about Pendergast exists.

The webpage makes claims concerning the *Long Island Medium* show that are incorrect.

~ The show doesn't get "the highest ratings of any cable television show in U.S. history." AMC's *The Walking Dead* boasts a far larger viewership. A fictitious show about what goes on "over there" *American Horror Story* ranks at 16. No TLC show is listed in the top 20 for 2012.
http://insidetv.ew.com/2012/12/12/this-years-most-watched-cable-shows/

~ Dr. Pendergast allegedly gave an interview to "The Guardian" in which he claimed that Ms. Caputo was "a fraud and a fake." There is no record of such an interview.

~ A second photo, a portrait of Sir Ken Robinson, is being passed off as Dr. James L. Pendergast.

~ Dr. Pendergast allegedly has THREE doctorate degrees: two from Harvard and one from Cambridge. No one by that name has ever received PhDs in social medicine or psychology, nor has anyone ever gotten both with that name. There isn't any record of anyone attending Harvard. Cambridge has no record of a James L. Pendergast receiving a PhD in physiology or attending the school. And there is no record of his alleged tutor, Raymond Josephson.

~ More bogus claims include his work appearing in dozens of scientific journals focusing on brain function and how it relates to emotional states.

~ Dr. Pendergast wrote a book called *The Long Kiss Goodnight* in 1987. We found no such book. Shane Black wrote a script called *The Long Kiss Goodnight* back in the 1990s but it wasn't about Africa. It was an action script made into a movie starring Geena Davis and Samuel L. Jackson.

~ The webpage claims that he won a Hugo Award for Outstanding New Fiction Author for a book called *The Hills Beyond Dublin* [a Steampunk novel]. No such award was ever given to this mythical book.

~ Dr. Pendergast allegedly lives in New Hampton, Connecticut with his wife and four children. We haven't located anyone that matches that data.

~ *The Theresa Caputo Diaries* will be 673 pages and has a tentative worldwide release of October 25, 2013. The publisher is Harvard Society Press. Not only doesn't the forthcoming book exist, neither does the publisher.

~ There are links for PayPal and another credit card company and if you click on them, you're taken to the main page, just as you are with NPR Books, Amazon, and B&N. They also give a reseller number, which is as bogus as the webpage.

So what can we say about this theresacaputofake.com page? What is the purpose of it?

~ It's just a joke. If so, it lacks any laughs. Real people and businesses are used and mocked. It jeopardizes their credibility.

~ Are they trying to swindle you to get $49.98? Possibly. However, you can't order it. Try sending an email and you'll get no response.

~ Is someone connected to Theresa Caputo's camp behind it? You know that old saying about no publicity is bad publicity ...

~ Is it a way to discredit the skeptics out there? Blogs like Eye on the Paranormal or websites like Scifake, and noted skeptic James Randi http://www.randi.org? Also, there are countless other bloggers who openly question the validity of Theresa's show and her claims. So the fake webpage creates confusion for critics and supporters alike.

Whatever the motive for this webpage, there are currently two eBooks about Theresa Caputo out there. Both are on Amazon for $1.99. One is 16 pages, the other a weightier 26 pages. They consist of rehashed information from copying and pasting internet articles and interviews on Theresa and her show.

Finally, we'll suggest that the creator of this page might have been inspired by this series of novels by Douglas Preston and Lincoln Child to help create the fake Dr. John L. Pendergast. Read more here:
http://en.wikipedia.org/wiki/Aloysius_Pendergast

Relic is the name of the first book in the Pendergast series:
http://www.amazon.com/Relic-Pendergast-Book-Douglas-Preston/dp/0812543262/ref=pd_sim_b_1

CHAPTER 15
FINAL THOUGHTS

Question: What's the difference between Theresa Caputo and Sylvia Browne?

Answer: About 30 years.

The center didn't hold the dam has broken the people have fled, and the outcome of the war is now in doubt.

Every author who writes a book thinks it'll change the readers' lives for the better. If it happens to be nonfiction, it just might change how people think. It may have such an impact the world will wake from a dream or a nightmare, and overnight we'll see a change.

I know this book doesn't fit that category. Those who needed to speak up about these issues years ago were asleep at the wheel. They should've been speaking out, the lawmakers of each state could've done something ... but didn't. Standing up to psychics/mediums that make false claims isn't appealing. It's not like hardliner issues that make headlines. Weeding out fakes doesn't serve as a main plank in a platform for an election.

Pastors and preachers should've spoken up as the cons filled their pockets. TV and radio show hosts got bigger ratings and filled their bank accounts. Publishers put out books knowing they should be classified as fiction or fantasy instead of nonfiction. They knew those far-out claims can't be validated. If any of the stuff within the books and DVD's were ever disproven, fans of new age teachers or psychics wouldn't allow their image to be tarnished. That new age teacher and author of ghostwritten pap sits by the pool enjoying the riches earned off the backs of the gullible public. They feed off the confused, those who search for something, grasping at everything and everyone that'll offer it to them blanketed in cotton candy clouds of lies. The preacher is more interested in the bottom line. The church could stand up to the onslaught of spiritual deceptions and cast them in a bad light. They don't. Why? Because seekers care about more hip and current issues like gay marriage, abortion rights and the controversial prayer in schools platforms. Those topics are politically popular and will get you in the news. Battling new age lies usually won't and even some pastors, so-called men and women of God, watched the new agers and learned about raking in the bucks. So, they put a Christian twist here and there and watched the profits roll in.

There was a time in this nation when men and women of the cloth were admired and looked up to. Doctors were respected; philosophers and writers were read to help keep people informed. Not anymore. We have the daytime talk show host who'll pimp that seer or new ager who claims they have the truth. People pay $200 for a ticket. They'll watch a scripted reality show and don't care about twenty-two minutes worth of entertainment sandwiched between tampon, fast food, toilet paper, and laxative commercials.

Some say we are in the end times. They say that the church, decency, truth, and honesty will crumble before the worst of the worst times. Maybe they're right.

God probably is crying a lot right now. Not to claim that I know what's on God's mind, but He is sad looking down from that heavenly city. He sees a world that had a Blessed Son offered to them. His Son paid the price of giving His life, His blood, and His body for it. Yet this world now turns to the likes of Theresa Caputo, John Edwards, Sylvia Browne, and James Van Praagh for spiritual answers. God gave us a teacher like Paul yet the world turns to reality TV show performers. The audience doesn't want wisdom, they want a bunch of made up stuff.

Christ was right -- we do not know what we do. Will we wake up in time?

CHAPTER 16
ABOUT THE AUTHOR

Author's Note:

Thank you for taking the time to read *Is the Long Island Medium the Real Deal?* Feel free to write a review on any of the online bookstores. Also, don't hesitate to tell your friends, family, and your local library about this book, along with my other titles!

Author's Bio:

Never one to mince words or afraid to speak what's on his mind, Kirby Robinson is either the most loved or the most hated man in the paranormal field.

Mr. Robinson has been a part of the paranormal field for over 25 years. His diverse background covers both the new age way of thinking and the Christian faith. He comprehends issues of ghosts, demons, hauntings, and demonic possessions, along with the occult and divination.

After accepting the call to become a demonologist, Mr. Robinson has traveled extensively in order to help individuals, families, and businesses confront and overcome demonic infestations, oppressions, and possessions. Mr. Robinsons has both assisted with and led exorcisms and deliverances. He has also done numerous house/office blessings and cleansings.

Mr. Robinson has managed the Eye on the Paranormal blog since September 2008. There are several different topics published each week, covering anything and everything paranormal and beyond.

On Wednesday nights, he hosts the two-hour long Eye on the Paranormal Radio Show on the God Discussion Network.

http://www.goddiscussion.net/2013/02/05/meet-the-hosts-kirby-robinson-eye-on-the-paranormal/

He is the author of:

Never Mock God: An Unauthorized Investigation into Paranormal State's "I Am Six" Case
[available in eBook and paperback formats]

Investigating Paranormal State Book 1

Is the Long Island Medium the Real Deal?

Paranormal State Exposed

Paranormal State: The Comprehensive Investigation

Paranormal Teachings: The Best of Shedding Some Light

LINKS:

Blog:
http://eyeontheparanormal.blogspot.com/

Radio Show:
http://www.goddiscussion.net/2013/02/05/meet-the-hosts-kirby-robinson-eye-on-the-paranormal/

Facebook:
https://www.facebook.com/kirbyjrobinson

Twitter:
https://twitter.com/eyeonparanormal

Amazon:
http://www.amazon.com/Kirby-Robinson/e/B004OKFI5Y

YouTube:
http://www.youtube.com/user/freeallspirits

Made in the USA
Monee, IL
25 May 2022